The Bad Girl's Guide to Getting Personal

The **Bad Girl's**

Guide to Getting Personal

by Cameron Tuttle

Illustrations by Susannah Bettag

CHRONICLE BOOKS
SAN FRANCISCO

Acknowledgments

Big wet thanks to all of the usual (and unusual) supsects for your bad influence. You know who you are and which ideas I've stolen. Bless you all. Props to the super baddies of the Swirl, www.badgirlswirl.com. I wish I had the space to thank each of you individually for your contribution to this book. And prime-time thanks to Steve and Jessica for my Hollywood home away from home. Love you, baby. Air kisses to all!

Text copyright © 2004 by Cameron Tuttle
Illustrations copyright © 2004 by Susannah Bettag
All rights reserved. No part of this book may be reproduced in any form without written permission from the publisher.

Bad Girl's Guide™ and Bad Girl Swirl™ are trademarks of Bad Girl Swirl, Inc.

Library of Congress Cataloging-in-Publication Data available.
ISBN 0-8118-4201-0

Manufactured in the United States of America
Designed by Pamela Geismar

Distributed in Canada by Raincoast Books
9050 Shaughnessy Street
Vancouver, British Columbia V6P 6E5

10 9 8 7 6 5 4 3 2 1

Chronicle Books LLC
85 Second Street
San Francisco, California 94105

www.chroniclebooks.com

You know it's time to start a relationship when Friday and Saturday night become

SEEKING . . . ME LOVE

Want to get personal with yourself?
Then I'm your girl.

SEEKING . . . GROUP LOVE

Dying to get personal with friends? You won't be disap-
pointed with us.

SEEKING . . . BIG LOVE

Aching to get personal with your romantic co-star? Who isn't, baby. Choose me!

Bad Girl Personals

SEEKING . . . TOUGH LOVE
Hoping to get personal with your family?
Dream on . . . er, rather, read on, baby!

SEEKING . . . CASUAL LOVE
Get personal with your crew—everyone's doing it!

ACTIVITY PARTNERS
Join in—we're tons of fun!

Me Love

Getting Personal with Yourself

Every bad girl has a personal secret—she's licensed to thrill!

When you're a bad girl, you know you've got the power—the power to bring people together and make them laugh, the power to find the fun in any situation, the power to get personal with anyone, anyplace, anytime.

Yikes! With great power comes great responsibility.

A true bad girl is not only in touch with her personal power, she's in control of it. She knows every minute of every day counts. Every word of every conversation makes a dent. Every person in every social swirl makes a difference. A bad girl always spots the opportunity to spread some love and make the world a badder place.

When you're getting personal every day in every way, you get what life is all about—putting more motion in your emotions, more hip in your relationships, and more action in your interactions. But to get personal, you've got to give personal. That means reaching out and touching people with your funny bone, your smarts, your quirky personality, and your unique sense of smile. It's about making every relationship in your life better and badder. With an attitude adjustment, you can unleash (or increase) your bad girl power and have a positively delicious effect on everyone you meet and greet.

laundry night. You know it's time to end a relationship when every other word he

Getting personal bad girl style is not always about getting intimate or getting naked, it's about getting real—real bold, real daring, real irreverent, real fun. You can get up close or get down and flirty. You can say and do the unexpected. You can play it for laughs or play for keeps. You can make amends or make trouble. You can melt away someone's emotional firewall with your charm and charisma or just get a stranger to crack a smile. However you choose to get personal in your relationships, be sure to add your own brand of bad.

Stop playing that good-girl mind game and set yourself

free. Just say adios to those boring insecurities, fears, and relationship worries that have been clogging your brain—then visualize beautiful, bad-iful you as the source of world peace! Remember you're only as hot and happening as you think you are.

Note to Self: Must be emotionally present to win!

says is, "What?" You know it's time to start a relationship when your mother

I've Got Me Love!

Any girl can (and should) feel self-love, but a bad girl feels that and so much more. She's got Me Love—a magical mix of self-respect and self-confidence, self-love and self-lust, self-style and self-starting fun. Me Love fuels your bad girl relationship engine. It gives you control of your body, your mind, and your social swirl. It gives you the courage to love whoever you want, however you want. It gives you the strength to say yes, no, or whoa in any relationship (even family!).

You Goo

You Goo is that voodoo that only you do so well. It's your sassy social lubricant. It's the thin layer of juice that conducts electricity and chemistry between you and everyone else in your world. You Goo doesn't make the relationship, it makes it badder. It's the grease that keeps the relationships in your life running smoothly. You Goo is your own personal blend of Baddy Sauce.

Drizzle it, spray it, say it, spritz it. When you shower the world with Baddy Sauce, you shower the world with love!

What Flavor Is Your Baddy Sauce?

Whatever flavor you choose, pour it on!

BBQ
hot and sour
picante
bittersweet chocolate
Béarnaise
syrup
ginger soy
marshmallow chewy
salsa fresca

sweet and nutty
honey pepper
green curry
horseradish
spicy meatball
lemon butter
catsup
jalapeño hot
plum duck

marries someone younger than you. You know it's time to end a relationship when

Living Badder Feels Better!

A good girl . . .	A bad girl . . .
plays it safe.	plays by her own rules.
sits back and waits.	gets out and dates.
keeps her guard up.	keeps the fun up.
always wants to fit in.	always wants to sleep in.
is bland and predictable.	is bold and irresistible.
lives up to other people's expectations.	lives for her own expectations.
never wants to be the freak.	always wants to be unique.
is afraid to speak her mind.	is afraid other people can read her mind.
thinks it's bad to be strong.	thinks it's strong to be bad..
would rather be liked than difficult.	would rather be loved and difficult.
is secretly growing bitter.	is openly growing better.
never questions authority.	never questions her gut vibe.
hopes a man will complete her.	knows a dirty martini will complete her.
avoids being selfish.	avoids eating shellfish.
feels guilty a lot.	feels a lot.
believes in compromising.	believes in living the dream.
is always polite.	is always provocative.

Do Something Bad!

What are you waiting for? An invitation? A break in the action? A personal timeout? Only good girls wait politely and watch the world go by. Bad girls make it happen. How do you want to go through life? How do you want to be remembered? Do you want to leave a mark? Or leave without anyone even noticing? Do you want to make the world a sadder place? Or make it a badder place?

Take a risk.
Reach out.
Run for office.
Start a trend.
Stop a wrong.
Start a business.
Start a revolution.
Sound an alarm.
Build a bridge.
Build an empire.
Take a stand.
Make a difference.
Break the rules.
Break the mold.
Go too far.
Go for broke.
Stay too long.
Speak your mind.
Lead a charge.
Leave a mark.
Take what's yours.
Be a social activist in all your relationships.

Note to Self: Indulge your hunger for delicious mischief at least three times a day.

he has to get drunk to get in the mood. You know it's time to start a relationship

More Bad Is Good

What's your personal Bad-o-Meter score?

Are you a social activist? Are you a political activist? Are you a style activist?

0	5	10
Total snooze	**Somebody's (a)muse**	**11 o'clock news!**

The Mood Pyramid

According to the USBAD, a bad girl does not rely on everyone else to supply all of the emotional nutrients she needs. She feeds her own self-esteem and feel-bad mood—with whipped cream and a cherry on top!

Bad girl's recommended daily mood diet

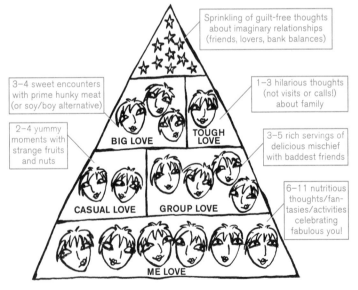

Sprinkling of guilt-free thoughts about imaginary relationships (friends, lovers, bank balances)

3–4 sweet encounters with prime hunky meat (or soy/boy alternative)

1–3 hilarious thoughts (not visits or calls!) about family

2–4 yummy moments with strange fruits and nuts

3–5 rich servings of delicious mischief with baddest friends

6–11 nutritious thoughts/fantasies/activities celebrating fabulous you!

BIG LOVE TOUGH LOVE CASUAL LOVE GROUP LOVE ME LOVE

Note to Self: Your brain is the ultimate power tool.

when you buy a wedding dress just because it was on sale. You know it's time to

Things to Do with . . . Condoms

(Use bright-colored, non-lubricated condoms unless otherwise indicated.)

* Pet galoshes

* Slip on each foot before showering at the gym or any frat house

* Cut off the tip, snip out two armholes, and make into a mod raincoat for Barbie!

* Lunchbox snack bags for carrots, cookies, or fruit

* Tie to the stem of your wineglass at parties so no one steals your glass

* Anti-theft, disposable cell phone case

* Open package, unroll, and drape on seatbacks to reserve your spot in crowded theaters when making a popcorn run

* Sassy garter belt/stash bag for formal events

* Fill two with Jell-O and pack in your bra for a Cheap-O boob job (If you get lucky, do a quick bait and switch. If you don't, you've got a late-night snack for the ride home.)

* Vibrator storage/travel bag

* Fill with Kool-Aid or juice and freeze (Makes a cool and refreshing Penis Pop!)

* Unroll a lubricated condom over each hand to moisturize hands and cuticles while watching movies at home

end a relationship when you realize you like his roommate more than you like him.

Bad Girl Rituals

Is your bad girl self feeling uptight and out-of-sight? No problem. It happens to the baddest of us. With a little behavior badification, she'll be back in a flash. Just recharge your bad girl battery with a few fun-filled daily rituals, alone or with friends. Your bad girl will be in tune and in the groove in no time. Revive, refine, and reclaim your inner wild to add some bad to your day.

Power Shake

It's the perfect way to start your day!

When you're getting ready in the morning, don't start thinking about business. Start your day thinking about badness! Crank a favorite personal power anthem, then dance around and shake your booty all the way through your morning routine. Who says you don't have time for fun? Remember: Fun-fest is the most important meal of the day!

Baddha Belly Pose & Meditation

Ideal for achieving winner strength and inner peace!

1. Change out of your clothes and into something revealing—or nothing at all.
2. Light a candle or two to set the mood.
3. Sit cross-legged in front of a mirror or your personal power shrine.
4. Gently clasp both hands under your Baddha belly, embracing it with love.

You know it's time to start a relationship when you start staying late at work

5. Close your eyes and breathe deeply into your belly.
6. In a soft voice, say, "Yummmmmmmm. Yummmmmmmm. Yummmmmmmm," and envision yourself in happy, healthy, badder relationships.

Repeat ten times or until you figure out what your relationship appetite is really craving.

Remember: An enlightened bad girl always makes time for a daily practice of self-worship—and shopping.

Primal Scream

Sometimes you just have to blow through your badness block with a healthy release of emotion. Whenever you feel the urge and spot an open window (car window, house window, window of opportunity), let it out! Whatever is pent up inside and giving you brain pain, hang out that window and release it! Shriek with agony, squeal with delight, or scream a not-so-secret primal dream. It's tons o' group-therapy fun when you do it with friends, casual acquaintances, or imperfect strangers!

Primal Scream Favorites:

"Ahhhhhhhhhhhhhhhhhhhhhh!"

"I'm bad as hell and not going to take it any more!"

"You can't make me!"

"I want it/him/sex now!"

"Where's my tiara?"

"Deal with it!"

"Don't change me—just love me!"

"Because I said so!"

"I want to *have* a baby, not date one!"

because it's fun. You know it's time to end a relationship when you say "Sorry" if

Bubbly Bath

Draw a hot bubble bath, add a splash of lavender oil, and pour yourself a cold glass of bubbly. Soak while you sip.

I'm So Hot Shower

Wash those negative thoughts down the drain as you soap up and worship every curve of your bodacious body. Be sure to appreciate every nook and cranny. When you get out of the shower, write a list of your baddest body parts on the steamy mirror.

I Candy

Before you can get personal with anyone else, you've got to get personal with yourself. Start by whispering sweet somethings to your reflection in the mirror, then repeat them whenever you're waiting in line, in traffic, or in bed. Things like . . .

"I am delicious and nutty!"

"I look good enough to eat!"

"I am chocolaty and chewy!"

"I am worth every calorie."

"I am sinfully sweet."

"I am 100-percent not fat-free!"

"I will melt in your mouth but not in your hands."

"I am bad and good for you."

you touch each other in bed. You know it's time to start a relationship when you

Play Make-Believe

It worked when you were five years old and guess what?
It still does! You'll feel so much better and badder when
you act out all of your wildest dreams and aspirations.
You're never too old to:

* go to the ball with the handsome prince.
* ride the shuttle to the moon.
* take your company public.
* give a brilliant acceptance speech when you win an
  Oscar/Emmy/Grammy/Tony/Baddy.
* host a tea party with your fabulously smart, savvy,
  and stylish new friends.
* patent another one of your brilliant, zany inventions.
* kiss . . .

    the TV.
    the prince.
    the princess.
    your new lover.
    your secret admirer.
    a mirror.
    a melon.
    your arm.

When you believe it can happen, dress for it, and practice
every day. You can make it happen!

are sick and he brings you chicken noodle soup. You know it's time to end a

Bad Girl Filter

Always trust the little voices in your head. They are your special little helper friends and your personal board of badvisors. They are your angels of delicious mischief. And they are talking to you for a reason. But occasionally, even what your little friends say must be refined so your brain can run badder. If you hear a voice that's judgmental, critical, bitchy, or good girl, simply run it through your Bad Girl Filter and proceed without caution.

Applying the Bad Girl Filter . . .

What Your Little Voices Say:

You are a total fraud.

Don't be too confident.

You shouldn't do this.

You're too ambitious to be feminine.

He'll never like me.

Your boobs are too small.

What You Hear Them Say:

You are a fabulous broad!

You can't be too confident.

You shouldn't do this without a cocktail.

You're too feminine not to be ambitious.

He'll never know enough to like me.

Your boots are too small. Buy another pair right now.

Don't eat that.

No one's looking; eat two!

You didn't deserve to win.

Don't forget to thank God, your agent, your lawyer, your publicist, and Mom.

Low-carb snacks.

Low-carb sex.

You drink too much.

You drink too much coffee.

You'll feel better if you do a little shopping.

You'll feel a lot better if you do a lot of shopping.

Better not give him your number.

Get his number.

You're going to feel so guilty.

You're going to feel so goood.

Don't kiss her.

Everyone's looking; kiss her twice!

Moderation at all costs.

You can't afford moderation at these prices!

He's going to break up.

What? Can't hear. You're breaking up!

They're gossiping about me.

They're gossiping about ME!

Note to Self: Just because you're single doesn't mean you're alone!

Going All the Way with Your Bod

If you think your body has to be perfect to be divine, then you are worshipping a false bod! Snap out of it! And snap your bad bootyful ass with this wet mental towel.

Being a bad girl is never about being perfect, it's about being real—the real you, all of you. It's about digging yourself, butt and all. A true bad girl is fearless but not flawless. That's what makes her so damn irresistible! So if you're afraid to jiggle when you giggle or bounce when you boogie, then you better get to first base fast.

1st Base: Making Peace with Your Body

Your body is always your best outfit. It's your birthday gift-wrapping. It's your home away from home. It's a one-of-a-kind, original piece of art. You can't leave it so you might as well love it—all of it.

Lie down on the sidewalk, a playground, or parking lot and get a friend to draw the outline of your body with colored chalk in a bunch of crazy positions. Return the favor until the asphalt looks like a crime scene.

2nd Base: Making Friends with Your Body

Face it. The relationships you build with your individual body parts will last forever. Get to know them, treat them like friends. Your boobs, butt, feet, nose, hair—whether too big, too small, too fat, too flat—are all in your personal posse. Go out and play with them and yourself. Always play hard with your body buddies but never be hard on them.

relationship when you would rather read a romance novel. You know it's time to

3rd Base: Making Love to Your Body

Get naked. Get comfortable, and let your fingers do the walking. Stop to take in the view of each glorious curve along your self-lover's lane. Cover your body in whipped cream, honey, or chocolate syrup and sprinkles—to celebrate not hide—the best parts. Then lap it up. Eat whatever you want without hestitation or guilt until you feel sexy and satisfied.

Home!

Slide into the sheets wearing nothing but Me Love. You're safe! Light a candle beside the bed, then sit back, and write your bod a steamy love letter. Don't be afraid to gush about every adorable detail and delicious dimple. Be sure to keep your growing stack of body love letters near the bed for late-night inspiration.

Note to Self: Curves are only dangerous when you go too fast.

start a relationship when you're so horny your parents' friends start looking hot.

Repackaging Your Package

Whether you're talking to someone else or talking to yourself, negative body language leads to negative body feelings. With a subtle attitude adjustment, you can build a relationship with your body parts based upon mutual love and respect. When you drop the put-downs and negative chatter, your body will feel better and badder.

Bad Body Language	Bad Girl Body Language
Don't look at my fat gut.	Worship my sexy, abundant Buddha belly.
I hate my flat chest.	I've got tasty lovin' spoonfuls.
My flabby arms are disgusting.	My hug flaps will smother you with love.
My skin is so pale.	Add my creamy complexion to your coffee, baby.
I hate my fat ass.	I've got tasty lovin' moonfuls!
My boobs are so huge.	My cups runneth over. Drink up!
I hate my sagging hips.	Ride 'em, cowboy. Saddle-bags are the new love handles!
I have skinny chicken legs.	I'm a free-range beauty.
My mustache is gross!	My lip shawl is soft and snuggly.
Just ignore my double chin.	My wattle is twice as nice.
My feet are way too big.	I am so grounded!

Note to Self: Acceptance is the key to thinner peace!

You know it's time to end a relationship when he forgets your birthday and he

Good Reasons to Be Kinda Fat

More is better, especially when it's more of you!
Embrace your baddy-licious bod and celebrate the
many good reasons to be big, bad, and beautiful.

* Sustains you in times of war

* No need to bring a sweater on cool evening dates

* Built-in life preserver

* Bigger boobs

* Sleep anywhere comfortably

* Last one to starve to death after the plane crashes
  in the Andes

* More of you to love

* Cradling the phone in your neck rolls means you
  can talk hands-free

* Don't have to wear a wetsuit

* Easy to keep a pen or pencil wedged between your
  thigh and butt cheek for collecting numbers at the
  beach or pool

Note to Self: Must become more of an imperfec-
tionist!

Improving Your Booty Image

Whether it's big and bouncy or small and mousy, whether it's wide and flat or round and fat, your booty deserves your unconditional love. Think about it! She is always there for you, supporting you through thick and thin. She covers your backside at work, at home, in the car, and at the bar. She is behind you 100 percent. No matter how wide, your butt never leaves your side.

When you're an authentic bad girl, your butt is your friend, your confidante, and your partner in crime. Isn't it time you show her some love? If you're kind to your butt, your butt will be kind to you.

Show Your Butt Some Love

* Send your butt flowers.
* Write a song about your butt and perform it at open-mike night.
* Let your butt feel the sun on its cheeks when at the beach or pool.
* Give your butt a sweet, tender nickname.
* Make a celebratory photo collage of your butt in various victory poses.
* When eating mashed potatoes, mold them into a glorious tribute to your shapely butt.
* Buy your butt a sexy new pair of jeans. (Sexy, but not too tight. Your butt has feelings too!)
* When soaping up in the shower, don't rush it. Relish it and spend some gentle quality time with your butt.
* Give your butt a sexy little swat when out on the town.
* Always refer to buttne as booty marks.

doesn't grovel. You know it's time to start a relationship when he calls to make

* Free your butt from the shame of a sweatshirt tied around your waist.
* Moisturize your butt cheeks morning and night with a gentle alpha hydroxy lotion.
* Embroider a sweet message to your butt on a seat cushion.
* Release your butt forever from heat-retaining, non-breathing polyester panties.
* Buy your butt a padded toilet seat.
* Organize a Butt Pride parade in your neighborhood.

Note to Self: Must make more Nude Year's Resolutions!

Positive Ass-firmations

Celebrate the unique beauty of your booty! Choose one of these positive ass-firmations (or create your own) and build a badder booty image. Say it loud and proud, alone or with friends.

No matter how wide, I've got super butt pride!
My butt's a delight 'cause she's filled with cellulite!
Small and tight, my butt is out of sight!
Jiggle, jiggle, jiggle, this butt was born to wiggle!
Dimpled and dreamy, my butt is cottage-cheese creamy!
My butt is delicious 'cause she's so bubble-icious!
Broad and flat, this butt is where it's at!
It's no rumor—my butt's got tongue-in-cheek humor!
I dig myself and my big butt shelf!
Step aside, my butt pride is double-wide!

Note to Self: The story of your butt has a very happy ending.

sure that you got home safe, and then he talks to you for three hours. You know

The Ten BAD Habits of Highly Seductive People

Rules, inhibitions, and men were meant to be broken.

Bad habits are meant to be cultivated and savored.

1. Be in love and in lust with yourself.
2. Dress inappropriately for all occasions.
3. Play with your hair.
4. Stare longer than you know you should.
5. Develop a sin/sin strategy and visualize making it happen.
6. Seductively stick out your tongue.
7. Stand a little too close to others.
8. Talk with your hands and punctuate with a touch.
9. Overshare personal details in a whisper.
10. Always eat dessert with a friend and your fingers.

it's time to end a relationship when you'd rather abstain than redo your hair

What's Sexy? You, Baby!

Sexy comes from within. It's your inner heat and your personal beat. And it's yours to own. Feeling sexy is not something anything or anyone can take away from you—not a guy, not a girl, not a magazine, not a scale, not a nasty comment from your inner bitch, your lover, or your mother. Sexy is all about you.

Sexy is . . .	**Sexy is not . . .**
a vibe	a size
being smart	playing dumb
following your path	following the pack
acting your age—and loving it	acting out your rage
hip action	acting hip
real confidence	real arrogance
relying on your instincts	relying on your looks
being comfortable in your skin	showing nothing but skin
dropping your emotional guard	dropping your standards
being real	being a real slut

Dating Yourself

It's not just for old farts anymore!

Before you can fall in love with someone else, you have to fall hard for yourself. And that can take time. So go ahead and start the long, luscious process of self-seduction. Explore what you like to do on a date and what you like about you on a date. Once you start dating yourself, you won't be disappointed. The company is fabulous, the conversation is scintillating, and the sex is yummy and calorie-free!

Delicious Ways to Date Yourself

First Date

Bust out the bubbly; you are going to impress yourself tonight! Start with a buzz and end with a little slap and tickle when you see how far you can get with yourself. Don't give it all away tonight—but if you do, you know you'll respect yourself in the morning.

* Blow on your own neck. Use your palm or a hand mirror to deflect your warm breath to all your exotic and erotic places.
* Take off your bra and let your girls have a real girls' night out.
* Slowly peel off your pants or skirt and slip into nothing more comfortable.
* Tickle yourself with a feather in your nethers until you don't feel like laughing anymore.

Movie Date

Rent a chick-flick double feature or a down-and-dirty NR art film. Either way, wear a skirt just in case you feel like

afterwards. You know it's time to start a relationship when you decide that

being naughty with the movie's hero in the dark.

* Buy some popcorn and seductively feed it to yourself. Be sure to use your tongue. Lick your buttery lips and laugh coyly when a piece "accidentally" tumbles into your cleavage.

* Lean down and use your tongue like a sexy serpent to retrieve it.

* Be sure to wear your remote-control vibrating panties so when things get steamy on screen, things can also get steamy in your own private I-da-ho.

* Hike up your skirt and whip your bare bottom with a Twizzler while sexily draping yourself over the seat in front of you.

Top Reasons to Date Yourself

* Saves money on makeup

* Helps pass the time during dry spells

* Safe sex

* That cold sore

* You know it's true love and it's going to last

* Makes your cat jealous and appreciate you more

* Never have to fake an orgasm (unless you're really neurotic!)

* Can answer, "Yes, Mom. I'm dating someone," with a straight face

showering every third day is important for water conservation. You know it's

Dinner Date

Glam it up, get your freak on, and head to the hippest bistro you know.

* Slink into a candlelit corner and pull out your compact. Make eyes at yourself and whisper about how the candlelight makes beautiful bonfires in your ocean-deep eyes.

* Order two glasses of champagne. Take one in each hand, then twist your arms together and sip seductively from both glasses . . . preferably at once.

* Order the lobster, kick off your shoes, and get *Flashdance* on your own ass. (Fold one leg under your body and wriggle around until your toes are doing the talking.) When you feel a little tipsy, take advantage of your lack of inhibitions and really get into your food. Put down your fork and feed yourself with your fingers. Lick each one clean to the delight of your inner Bad. Savor each morsel and be sure to be vocal about how pleasing it all is. And don't skimp on the wine.

* Hold your own hand or any other body part you're attracted to. Gentle stroking of the inner palm (among other things) can get your desert juices flowing.

Study Date

Smart is the new sexy, so hit the library or bookstore. Poke your head into whatever interests you. Just try not to knock anyone over with your giant brain.

time to end a relationship when you decide that you'd rather use the extra

* Distract yourself from studying by doodling love notes to yourself in the margins of your notebook.
* Write down your phone number and covertly slide it across the table. Then run to the other side to get it and smile secretly when you read it.
* Meet yourself in the romance section for a re-enactment of some Danielle Steele steam scene. Don't be coy. You know you want it, otherwise you wouldn't have shown up! Push yourself up against the bookshelf and grope yourself a little harder than you meant to.
* Let your late-night coffee cool from scalding to hot, and place the cup snugly between your legs. The warmth of the coffee bean will penetrate your soul as "caffeine euphoria" takes on a whole new meaning.

Gym Date

Sure, you probably think of the gym as a sweaty, smelly place, but that doesn't have to be a bad thing. (Imagine your bedroom after a really hot date!)

* Pick up a couple of free weights and kiss your biceps with every curl. This will keep your arms and your lips nicely toned. Be sure to watch your every move in the mirror.
* Spinning class is today what washing-machine spin cycles were to the fifties. Strap on your sneakers and leave the gel seat at home. There's more than one reason to pedal harder.
* Pinch your own ass as you walk past the water fountain.
* Get buck wild in the hot tub. Press up to the jets. Those babies can do a lot more than massage your back.

water than shower together. You know it's time to start a relationship when

Group Love

Getting Personal with Friends

When you're living the bad life, you know the best relationships are the ones you share with your personal posse of bad girl friends—better known as Group Love.

Your bad girl friends know the real you and love you anyway. They bring out the best in you and aren't afraid to get up close and personal with the baddest of you. Bad girl friends are the real deal. They don't want some pre-fab, no-flab, blow-up friend, they want you—fab flaws, crazy quirks, and all. Bad girl friends feel an unconditional, untraditional love—their only expectation is that you be true to yourself and true to your friendship. Spending QT with your BG's is always a shake-up call—reminding you who you really are and what you really want out of life.

A bad girl friend is more than a play date, she's your very own personal manager. She helps you navigate those tricky career moves, dicey dating decisions, and crucial wardrobe choices. Bad girl friends are pushy in a good way, encouraging you to push the envelope, push your expectations, and push yourself to live your wildest, wackiest dreams. They push you to be the better, badder you. A true bad girl friend will never let you down and never, ever let you settle for living the safe life, dating the dull guy, or staying trapped in some dead-end job. It's a

you know all the reality TV personalities by their first names. You know it's time

bad girl friend's duty to drop-kick your booty out of your safety zone and into your bad girl groove, inspiring and conspiring in delicious mischief along the way.

Your bad girl friends are always there for you. They're your underwire support group, joining forces to lift your life and give it a well-rounded, perky appearance, even when you might be sagging a bit beneath the surface. A true bad girl friend listens like a shrink but never watches the clock. If she sees you getting stuck in a rut, she's right there to light a fire under your butt. She takes on your problems like they're her own and provides you with a kick-ass bad girl prescription every time.

Bad girl friends always remind each other to live the bad life—squeezing the most fun out of every day and loving each one like it was your first.

Note to Self: Bad girl friends like your outer cool, but love your inner fool.

Say NO to:	Say GO to:
back stabbing	butt patting
ego trips	road trips
self-destructive behavior	self-constructive behavior
being bitchy	being bold
judgment calls	wake-up calls
being mean-spirited	being team-spirited
bringing you down	getting down
insult swapping	shoe swapping
boredom	stardom
being lame	being game

to end a relationship when he feels threatened by your celebrity crushes.

Mutual Badmiration Society

The best bad girl posses are like a mutual badmiration society—dishing out compliments, patting backs, stroking egos, and spreading the bad girl butter on thick. It's a win-win, group-love-in, and a constant reminder that you're all beautiful, bold, brilliant, and bad . . . just the way you are.

To experience the mutual pleasures of true group love, all the baddies in your posse must agree that it's one for all and all for fun. Each groupie has to feel the love, play her position to the baddest of her ability, and be there to support the other members of the team. Through thick and through thin—when other friends wimp out—your baddies are always in.

Not only will your bad girl friends supply you with all the group love and support you need, but they count on you to dish it right back, no questions asked. And just like those treasured Big Love romantic relationships, your bad girl friendships need to be nurtured and nuzzled to grow and thrive, stay happy and alive. While your hot romance might fizzle or flop, your bad girl friends will stick around.

Note to Self: Buy semi-sweet chocolate chips for next bad girls' night in.

Bad Girl Friendship Vows

Every bad girl friendship has its own unique rhythm and unspoken set of rules and regulations. But underneath it all, there are certain cornerstones that are non-negotiable. They're the friendship foundation upon which you build your house of bad girl fun. Just like wedding vows seal the holy covenant of marriage, bad girl vows seal the holy fun-event of your friendship. If you can't look her in the eye and say these words from the bottom of your heart, then it may be time to reassess the relationship.

Place your left hand on this book, lovingly cup your left breast with your right hand, and say these vows aloud:

I vow to love the whole you and nothing but you, so help me Bad Girl.

I vow to take you seriously and remind you not to take life too seriously.

I vow to bring out the baddest in you—every day, in every way.

I vow to tell you the truth, even when it hurts.

I vow to honor your boundaries (unless it's obvious that you don't want me to).

I vow to listen to you and give my best advice, but never to preach or judge.

I vow to cover your ass—but never covet it.

I vow never to let you settle for anything less than the bad life.

When you complete your vows, you may read (or sing or rap) this passage aloud in unison: *By the powers vested in this book by the Mutual Badmiration Society, we now pronounce us best bad girl friends. We may now kiss each other's sweet booties!*

You know it's time to start a relationship when you apply to be on a reality TV

Things to Do with . . . Pantyliners

* Conversation-starter bookmark, perfect for reading in libraries, cafes, or on public transportation

* Blot lipstick

* Stick one to the back of each hand for stay-put napkins at BBQ buffet

* Blindfold for impromptu bondage games

* Polish fine silver

* Crimp in the middle and wear as a bowtie when crashing formal affairs

* Tape his mouth shut

* Stick over ears at family gatherings to block out critical comments and earn instant "crazy relative" status

* Spell out "I Love/Miss/Hate You" on his or her car windshield

* Adhere to thigh and discreetly take notes during first dates

* Use two on each nipple for floral-shaped pasties

* Configure three into a quickie Princess Bad Girl tiara and stick to your head

* Write specific diving directions for your love muffin and adhere just above your bikini line

* Decorate with rhinestones and glitter to make fab femme-power cuff bracelets

* Purse-sized lint roller

show. You know it's time to end a relationship when he blocks your e-mail

Living Wills and Won'ts

Once you've got the basics of your individual friendships covered, the rest is group love gravy. Gather the baddies in your posse and draft up your own Living Wills and Living Won'ts: a customized checklist of the things you will and won't do for—and to—each other. Be sure all points are clearly spelled out, all parties are in compliance, and every baddy is ready to sign on the dotted line.

Here are a few examples to get you started:

Living Wills	Living Won'ts
I will slowly drive by your crush's house while you crouch on the floor of my car.	I won't honk the horn.
I will remember your birthday and do something about it.	I won't tell anyone how old you really are.
I will admit when you're right.	I won't ever say "your mother's right."
I will remind you to stand up for yourself.	I won't judge you if you don't.
I will accept your decisions.	I won't accept any lame excuses.
I will tell you when you're being an impossible bitch.	I won't write off your emotional intensity as PMS.

address. You know it's time to start a relationship when you fill out a job

Living Wills	Living Won'ts
I will tell you how your butt really looks in those.	I won't borrow your favorite jeans if my butt looks better in them.
I will tell you when you have a booger hanging out of your nose.	I won't tell you how to live your life.
I will help you analyze the message he left on your machine.	I won't screen your calls.
I will laugh loudly at your dorky jokes so people think you're funny.	I won't laugh at your big-time dreams.

The Bad Girl Variety Show

Variety is the spice of the bad girl life. That's why every baddy in your posse should have her own unique style and trademark schtick—kind of like that great ensemble cast on your favorite sketch comedy show (think *Saturday Night Live, Mad TV, Whose Line Is It Anyway?*). The most talented casts shine because they strike a perfect balance of personalities who work overtime to support each other's unique gifts. The beauty of an ensemble cast is that every baddy gets her turn in the spotlight, but in the end, the whole cast hits the stage together for a big group-love bow.

When you start planning auditions for your own Bad Girl Variety Show, consider the different roles each of your baddies plays best and then cast your co-stars accordingly.

application and write "Googling people" under hobbies. You know it's time to

Bad Girl Co-Stars

The Go-Star

Her On-Stage Schtick The queen of improv who can take any cue and go with it—dishing out on-the-spot one-liners that are funnier than anything in the script.

Her Off-Stage Trick An innate ability to talk her way onto guest lists, out of speeding tickets, and into the game without batting an eye.

The "Just Say No" Star

Her On-Stage Schtick The executive editor who knows which acts are a go and which ones are a no. She makes the decisions nobody cares or dares to argue with and always manages to cut the crap and get the laughs.

Her Off-Stage Trick Helps everyone in the posse edit her personal good girl calendars, cutting out unnecessary work engagements, family functions, and blind dates to make way for mandatory bad girl fun.

The "In The Know" Star

Her On-Stage Schtick The naughty news anchor with the witty social commentary, brilliant political observations, and sarcastic spin on the daily news.

Her Off-Stage Trick Heats up cocktail party conversation with her hilarious spin on what's happening in the world, getting everyone in the room to start quoting NPR.

The Ha Star

Her On-Stage Schtick The hottie who always gets to play the sex kitten, hypnotizing the audience with her assets and then pulling the rug out from under them with her slapstick comic brilliance.

Her Off-Stage Trick Flashes her pearly whites and perky cleavage to get the group past the velvet rope and into the VIP lounge where she drops the pretty-girl act, dances on tables, and moons the DJ.

The Whoa! Star

Her On-Stage Schtick The ultimate risk taker who's not afraid to wear the wackiest get-ups, look ugly, and body slam the set, risking injury and bad hair to get a good laugh.

Her Off-Stage Trick Inspires every baddy to let go of trying to look perfect and, instead, wear that crazy outfit and let her inner goofball out to play.

The Show Star

Her On-Stage Schtick The guest star of the week, who gets worked into every skit, keeping the show fresh and new.

Her Off-Stage Trick Typically an out-of-towner, this wild card pops in for the weekend and infuses the crowd with fresh new energy.

Are You a Bad Girl Friend? (A Quiz)

1. My idea of bad girl bonding is
_____.
A. shoe shopping and a healthy, low-carb brunch
B. vibrator shopping and a lengthy, tell-all lunch
C. spontaneously road-tripping to the desert, eating peyote with a shaman, and joining a commune of cactus worshippers for a day

2. When my bad girl friend and I are both feeling stuck in a rut, I sign us up _____.
A. for a pottery class at the co-op
B. for amateur belly-dancing night at the Hookah Palace
C. as volunteers in a well-paid experimental study testing the effects of Viagra on women

3. If I were in a lingerie store and saw my bad girl friend's favorite thongs on sale, I'd
_____.
A. make a mental note and mention it the next time we talk
B. put one in every color on hold for her under the name Ms. Cheeks
C. buy her one in every color and hire a cute bike messenger to rush them to her office in a clear plastic package addressed to Sweet Cheeks

4. When my bad girl friend seems totally stressed and depressed, I take her _____.
A. to a day spa for a calming Swedish massage
B. to the candy store to calmly gorge on Swedish fish
C. to the airport, get in the shortest line, get out the credit card, and see where we end up

5. The last time my bad girl friend got pulled over for speeding while I was riding shotgun, I _____.
A. started to cry and begged him not to give her a ticket
B. flashed some thigh and nibbled her ear suggestively, distracting him from writing a ticket
C. stuffed my jacket under my shirt, splashed some Evian on my pants, and panted, "Oh my God! My water just broke!," inspiring a full-siren police escort

6. When my bad girl friend hooked up with her ex again, I asked her _____.
A. how she could have done such a stupid thing
B. if she had any regrets
C. if she had an orgasm

7. The last time my bad girl friend and I were flat broke on a Friday night, I suggested we
_____.
A. stay home and give ourselves pedicures
B. stay home and give ourselves vacuum-nozzle hickeys
C. put on tutus and roller skate from neighborhood bar to bar, setting up shop in a corner booth and offering mini manicures in exchange for martinis

end a relationship when you catch him bidding online for hot pink pumps in

8. At least once in the past, I've made my bad girl friend laugh so hard she _____.
A. did the pee-pee dance
B. actually peed in her pants
C. peed in her pants while sitting on someone's lap

9. The last time my bad girl friend had a flight arriving at rush hour, I _____.
A. offered my deepest condolences
B. offered the name and number of a great shuttle service
C. showed up at the airport dressed as a mime and communicated only with nonverbal, full-body sign language until we got to my car

10. If I found out my bad girl friend's boyfriend was cheating on her, I'd _____.
A. look the other way and pretend it wasn't happening
B. look her in the eye and tell her the truth
C. look him in the eye and tell him what he could do to himself

11. If my bad girl friend fell for a guy I once dated (and was over), I'd _____.
A. tell her to go for it and then secretly feel weird
B. tell her to go for it and that I think it's a weird move
C. tell her what his favorite weird moves are in bed

12. When my bad girl friend got ditched at the altar, I _____.
A. quietly thanked god that it wasn't me
B. thanked him with my knee
C. grabbed her hand and lead her skipping down the aisle yelling "Free at last!"

Wanna Be Bad

If you answered A to most questions, you're a good friend, but not a bad girl friend. You tend to play it safe and somewhat selfish, which doesn't allow for proper bad girl bonding on a deeper, more decadent level. To take your friendship to the next level, loosen up and let her in—you'll be amazed how much better and badder your friendships can be when you go the extra mile and let the bad times roll. *Assignment: Review the Bad Girl Friendship Vows on page 38 and work on putting those bad ideas into action.*

Gonna Be Bad

If you answered B to most questions, you're so close to being the ultimate bad girl friend that you can taste it (and it sure is sweet). You're willing to accept your baddies for who they are and revel in the unbearable badness of being friends. To bump it up to the next level, remember to think outside the box, push her envelope, and demonstrate badness in your everyday actions. *Assignment: Review the Breast Friend Exam checklist on page 46 and vow to check off one new activity a day.*

Gotta Be Bad

If you answered C to most questions, you are the baddest girl friend of them all. You always go the extra mile and do it with naughty, bad girl style. You're fiercely loyal to your friends and a living, breathing example of what it really means to be bad. *Assignment: Make more delicious mischief and keep up the bad work!*

size 11. You know it's time to start a relationship when you look forward to seeing

The Breast Friend Exam

You've seen each other at your best, your worst, and your baddest. You've been there together, done that as a duo, and lived to tell the story to a captive audience over cocktails. You're the breast of bad girl friends. Or so you think.

To check up on the true state of your bond and be sure it's as healthy and well-rounded as you believe it to be, fill out Dr. Bad Girl's friendship form below. Check off the things you and your bad girl friend have done together and then let the doctor do the rest. Remember, no matter how healthy your friendship may seem, you should perform self—breast friend exams at home on a regular basis, mentally fondling your friendship to be sure it's growing in a healthy way and developing as quickly as you'd like it to.

Have you and your bad girl friend . . .

__ road-tripped cross-country?
__ done donuts in the parking lot at lunch?
__ covered each other's butts at work?
__ shown each other your respective butt tattoos?
__ seen each other throw a tantrum at the DMV?
__ seen each other throw up?
__ done the bad girl dance in your undies in front of the mirror?
__ done the bad girl dance in your undies in front of an audience?
__ seen each other pee beside the road?
__ seen each other pee in your pants?
__ shared a boyfriend?
__ shared a secret?
__ shared a bed?

the mailman more than the mail. You know it's time to end a relationship

___ talked your way out of a speeding ticket?
___ talked your way into an exclusive premiere?
___ borrowed her toothbrush?
___ borrowed her thong?
___ slept with the same guy?
___ slept with the same girl?
___ given her a home bikini wax?
___ given her name out as your emergency contact?

Give yourself a point for each activity checked and see where you rank.

[16-20 points] Breast of Friends

The two of you are like a double scoop of delicious trouble. Your friendship is vivacious, voluptuous, and as deep as Dolly's cleavage. There's nothing you haven't seen each other do and nothing you wouldn't do for each other. Continue to let the badness bounce and add your own daring adventures to this list.

[13-15 points] Bosom Buddies

You're like two wonderfully codependent orbs of loving goodness suspended in perfect push-up bra harmony, complimenting each other and turning heads wherever you go. Some people may say that you're inseparable—and they're right! Together you stand, divided you fall apart.

[9-12 points] Blossoming Beautifully

You're on the path to a fully developed friendship. Together, you make a perky and uplifting team. At the

when you get more excited seeing the in-laws than seeing him. You know it's

rate you're going, you'll be busting the buttons of your friendship and collecting popcorn kernels in no time. Everyone is very excited to watch the two of you grow together without growing apart.

[5–8 points] Naughty Nipples

Keep up the hard work, continue to make your point, and enjoy the perks of this slowly developing friendship. If you need a reminder of why you're friends, try pinching yourself to perk things up.

[2–4 points] Sagging Sacks

Your relationship is hanging heavy and low and is crying out for a lift. Try some extra support from your baddest friends or a visit to the baddy surgeon for a simple nip and tuck.

[0–1 points] Busted Flat

Your relationship is as flat as two silver-dollar pancakes. Consider fluffing it up with some bad girl bonding activities, accept that it's just not going to rise and enjoy it anyway, or make like a bra and snap out of it.

Don't Be Fooled by Breast-of-Friend Implants!

They try to trick you into thinking they're the real deal with perky compliments, bouncy premature terms of endearment, and false intimacy. Watch out—they're totally fake and full of silicone!

time to start a relationship when you pull a muscle masturbating. You know it's

Telltale Faux-Friend Behavior:

* She only includes you in group plans—never one on one.

* She keeps saying, "That's so you!" the first time you ever hang out.

* She has no idea where you were born.

* She puts on a big lovey-dovey show, but disses you when the crowd thins.

* When something very upsetting is going down in your life, she cuts you off halfway through with an air hug, and says, "Chin up, it will all work out!"

* She invites you to her birthday/ bachelorette/housewarming party because she wants your gift more than your company.

* She gushes over your "new" haircut when you haven't been to the salon for months.

* She tries to set you up on a blind date and has no idea you're taken.

* She calls you "sweetie" and air-kisses you the second time you get together.

Bad Girl Bondage

True bad girl friends share much more than racy good times and ridiculous adventures. You share a burning desire to improve your lives, expand your horizons, increase your bank balances, and amaze the world in the process. To strengthen your baddy bonds, you've got to share activities that stoke your mutual fires and stimulate those big, bad brains. The right bonding club will bring you and your co-baddies closer to your goals, closer to your dreams, and closer to each other.

Bad Girls Garden Club

A great excuse to get outside, slip into gaudy floral short-shorts, and strike a seductive pose as you bend over to prune your petunias. If you don't have a green thumb, don't worry! This club isn't so much about cultivating a garden as it is about cultivating a good time in a lush natural setting. Set up a circle of lawn chairs in the garden (or a park) with a posse of fresh bad girls and a tray of refreshing drinks and revel in the botanical pleasures of the great outdoors. If the weather heats up enough, hose down the Slip 'N Slide or fill up the wading pool and make a splash in your neighborhood. Extra points for pool hopping and naked Slip 'N Slide face plants.

Bad Girls Titillating Tupper-Wear Party

At a traditional Tupperware party, the host invites friends to sample a wide variety of storage container possibilities. Each guest places orders and goes home with a stack of useful new kitchen accessories. At a bad girl Tupper-wear party, guests must provide their own Tupperware containers filled with various titillating surprises—a lacy thong, a key-chain vibrator, scandalous Polaroids, hot pink pasties. Guests must choose a closed container at random, open it to reveal the naughty surprise inside, and then tell the group in delicious detail what they plan to do when they rush home. The baddest bad girl confession gets to host the next party.

Note to Self: Edible undies stay fresher in an airtight container kept in the fridge— and you stay fresher in no undies!

Bad Girls Memoir Writing Club

Who puts the "me" in memoir? You do, baby! Organizing a group of baddy scribes is a wonderful way to express yourself and share your bad girl stories in a supportive, creative environment. This is no time to hold back. Make your story as racy, raunchy, real, and revealing as you want, setting the record straight once and for all. (When you become famous, your many biographers will thank you!) Just be sure to change the names of the innocent— and the guilty—to protect their reputation and your inheritance. Remember, writing well is the best revenge! Title ideas: *Mi Vida Mala, Angela's Asses, Confessions of a Dirty Mind, Memoirs of a Bad Girl, Blue Velveteen Rabbit, My Left Foot Fetish, The Bitches of Madison County, Under the Tuscan Son, My Life as a Frog, Ho for the Holidays, Free to Pee You and Me.*

Note to Self: Remind family etc. it's never too late for hush money.

reach for it. You know it's time to start a relationship when you start reading spam

Bad Girls Naughty Knitting Circle

What bad girl doesn't crave creative expression and a healthy outlet for her obsessive-compulsive tendencies? Organize a group of crafty bad-dies who are dying to learn a new skill and let the knitting needles fly. Instead of making the same old boring hats and scarves, think outside the ball of yarn and whip up a few foxy, one-of-a-kind creations for everyone you love. Pattern suggestions: a naughty chenille thong for your best friend, a rasp-berry beret for your bad girl mom, cashmere handcuffs for your boyfriend, a wool bikini top for your cat, an elf hat for your Chihuahua.

Bad Girls Sin-vestment Club

Every bad girl wants and deserves financial independ-ence—creating a savvy, sassy investment strategy is the fastest way to get it. All you need are a few like-minded baddies with some spare change in their pockets and dollar signs in their eyes. Get the group together, pool your resources, invite a bad girl financial advisor, and start building your big, bad portfolio. Instead of investing in the same old stuffed-suit stocks, spice up your portfo-lio with the super sin tax test. Look for companies that offer delicious goods and naughty services that support and sweeten the bad girl lifestyle (always thriving during a down economy when everyone is depressed and/or self-medicating!). Then research, buy low, and sell high! Who knew financial planning could be so much fun? Sin companies to explore: Krispy Kreme, Starbucks, TiVo,

Nestlé, eBay, Tiffany & Co., Tanqueray, Saks Inc., Playtex.

Bad Girls Drama Club

Bad girls thrive on good drama and bad performances just as much as anyone else does. Forming a Bad Girl Drama Club is the perfect excuse for you and your friends to express your inner rage through alter egos. Come dressed as your favorite drama queen (think Bette Davis, Joan Collins, your evil stepmother) and take turns strutting around the room, blowing off steam and blowing your problems way out of proportion. Activities include: throwing hissy fits, storming around in tears, ranting, raving, whining, stomping feet, and hurling the occasional piece of valuable glassware across the room while screaming "Why, God, why? Why me?" Be sure to give a Baddy Award to the best drama mama!

Bad Girls Book Club

Get a group of stimulus-starved brainy babes together and choose a classic or a classic piece of chick lit (written by a chick, starring a chick) that you were forced to read in high school or college—and hated. This time, rename the novel and rewrite the most boring scenes with an all-new bad girl twist, transforming your heroine into a hardcore bad girl who talks the talk and walks the walk. Be sure to act out the best new scenes. Suggested titles: *The Color Pink, Anne of Green Fables, Little Whippin', The Hot Pink Letter, Bad Girl Pride Without Prejudice, The Ili-bad, Jane Rear, Ethan Foam, For Whom the Belle Throbs, Withering Hots, To the White House.*

out other girls . . . or guys. You know it's time to start a relationship when you

Plagued Personas: Bad Friend Management

We all know at least one of these characters. They're those problem friends that we tend to keep in our inner circle even when their bad behavior is out of control. Why do we let them linger in our lives and when should we cut them loose? It's all a matter of perspective.

Judge Prudy

The attitude: Smile tightly and carry a big gavel.

The dirty deed: Passes judgment on your bad girl lifestyle.

The secret need: To live your bad girl lifestyle.

Why you let it go: She's the only person who still worries about you.

When to say no: The second she makes you start worrying about yourself.

I La Blow

The attitude: Anything you say or do may be used in a conversation against you.

The dirty deed: Knows your weak points and hits below the belt.

The secret need: She's a sinking ship of insecurity and wants to take you down with her.

Why you let it go: She turns you into a sinking ship of insecurity that feels guilty not going down with her.

When to say no: Right now—before you drown in low self-esteem.

Barfa Stewart

The attitude: If it's not perfect, it's not worth it.

The dirty deed: She's such a phony perfectionist, she makes you want to barf.

The secret need: To control the world by starching and folding all the underwear.

Why you let it go: She starches and folds your underwear.

When to say no: She starts to starch your style.

Scameron Diaz

The attitude: Oops, I took it again!

The dirty deed: "Borrows" your favorite earrings, lip gloss, CDs, and sweaters without asking and denies it when confronted.

The secret need: An irrational urge to steal back what she seems to think the world owes her.

Why you let it go: Because she gives much more than she takes. (And she makes you feel so together!)

When to say no: You feel like you can't leave her alone in your room.

Me-Me Rogers

The attitude: Enough about me, back to me.

The dirty deed: She has no interest in anything but herself.

The secret need: For someone to find her interesting and love her.

Why you let it go: She is interesting—and great material for your stand-up act.

When to say no: She makes you feel like you're not.

Jealous Joplin

The attitude: Why's it always Marsha, Marsha, Marsha?

The dirty deed: So jealous of you that she can't be happy for you.

The secret need: To be you.

Why you let it go: It feels pretty good to be envy-worthy.

When to say no: When even you can't be happy for you anymore.

Dear Blabby

The attitude: If it's syndicated, it's vindicated.

The dirty deed: She blabs your business to everyone.

The secret need: To lure friends by offering the sordid details of other people's lives.

Why you let it go: She's your number-one gossip source.

When to say no: You wonder what she says when you're not around.

The Bad Girl Fair Trade Agreement

Bad girl friends share a lot of things—great clothes, juicy gossip, deep secrets, big dreams. It's a win-win tradeoff that doubles your wardrobe and doubles your fun, without tripling your credit card bill or crippling your style.

Sharing your stuff with your bad girl friends is like sharing your life with them. When you wear a friend's clothes, you get to be like her for the night—borrowing her bad attitude, bad one-liners, and bad dance moves. When you lend stuff to a friend, you get to live vicariously through her—experiencing the next morning everything she and your little black tube top did the night before.

It's only fair. And it's only stuff.

Swapping clothes, accessories, jewelry, and even men with your posse reminds you that *you* dial your personal style. It comes from who you are, not what you wear. It's not the skirt that makes you sexy—it's how you move and groove when you wear it. It's not the bag that makes you hip—it's the way you carry it and carry yourself. It's not the boots that make you strong and stylish—it's where and how far you're going in those boots. And it's not the lipstick that makes you irresistibly kissable—it's what you say and how you say it. No matter whose clothes you're wearing, the You Goo shines though.

In a perfect world, the give and take between friends would be silky smooth and snag-free. But let's face it—perfection is overrated and boring. So a few guidelines are in order. It's an unspoken Bad Girl Fair Trade Agreement that helps you monitor the cross-bad-girl-border movement of goods and services, opening closet doors and dresser drawers nationwide.

sleep with the TV on all night for the company. You know it's time to end a

If not done correctly, unsupervised borrowing and lending can lead to confusion and nasty catfights. To avoid this unnecessary strife, simply follow the golden rule and apply these commandments to your trading life:

* Shoe unto others as you would like them to shoe unto you.
* Do unto her cashmere sweater as you would like her to do unto yours.
* Dry clean her belongings as you would like her to dry clean your own.
* Ask very nicely and ye shall usually receive. If not, try bartering. (Then begging.)
* Thou shalt not worship false knock-offs.
* If thou breaketh the heel, thou shall buyeth the shoe.
* Thou shalt return items on time, every time. Late fees are double on new releases.
* Thou shalt return items in the same condition they were in when you borrowed them.
* Thou shalt not covet thy neighbor's crocodile clutch, though you may ask to borrow it.
* Thou shalt not leave cakey white pit-prints all over her black top.
* If thou stain it, thou must explain it with a detailed account of how it happened. (Extra points for live re-enactments or candid Polaroids that capture the event on film.)

relationship when passing gas is foreplay. You know it's time to start a

The No-Act Pact

Healthy friendships have healthy boundaries, especially around men. A true bad girl never lets a man come between her and a girlfriend. (Unless, of course, it's a three-way between consenting adults!)

When there's a hot guy friend in your social swirl, a guy you and all of your friends would love to love, then it's time for a No-Act Pact. This U.N. (United Notions) Peace Agreement establishes the boundaries so that everyone in the group can be close, have fun, and stay friends. Nobody gets him—and nobody gets hurt. It's important to spell out the terms of the pact and agree to them in advance when everyone is calm, cool, and not crying. Seal the deal with a drop of blood, a suck of helium, a shot of tequila, or all of the above.

Whether or not you tell the guy that he's covered by a No-Act Pact is up to you and the kind of guy you're dealing with. It's nicer to be up-front and let him know but much more amusing to let him ho—and get nowhere!

Note to Self: Friends don't let friends dive drunk.

Proposed No-Act Pact Guidelines

1. You can kiss him on the cheek—but not on the lips.
2. You can go to a movie together—but not to a sexy movie.
3. You can hold his hand—but you cannot place it on your breast.
4. You can take him as your date to a family wedding—but you cannot enjoy it.
5. You can sit next to him on a sofa—but you cannot sit on him, anywhere.
6. You can fantasize about him—but you cannot tell him.
7. You can cry on his shoulder—but you cannot accidentally suck his neck.
8. You can see him in a bathing suit—but not in the raw.
9. You can share a hot tub—but not a hot bath.
10. You can dance with him—but not bump and grind or rub your ass in his crotch.
11. You can ask him to lift heavy stuff for you—but not ask him to lift your skirt.
12. You can call him late at night—but not if you're crying or drunk.

Dating Tip: If you and a friend (or group of friends) can't decide who gets first dating dibs on a new piece of sweet meat, then simply organize a quick ro-sham-ho. Think Rock, Paper, Scissors. Winner dates all!

relationship when massaging a hamstring cramp gets you hot. You know it's

The Bad Girl Barter System

In the bad girl free-for-all market, bartering for goods and services is a healthy, economical way for you and your friends to give and get what you need and want—trading this for that, tit for tat. It's a "you scratch my back, I'll scratch yours" proposition and a bad girl's get-itched-quick scheme that really works. If you're not sure what your tits (products) and tats (services) are worth on the bad market, brush up on the current exchange rates. Then get creative and get bartering!

Current Bad Girl Market Exchange Rates

Tit	Tat
one MAC lipgloss	one late-night run for Big Macs
one pair of strappy heels	one Happy Meal
one pair of slinky stilettos	one foot massage
one cap-sleeve T-shirt	one cappuccino
one leopard-print stole	one weekend of cat-sitting
one faux fur bag	one weekend of Shih Tzu sitting
one pair of Manolos	one pack of Marlboros
one hot pink miniskirt	one hot meal
one baby-blue mohair sweater	one night of baby-sitting
one cowboy hat	one shot of whiskey
one pair of cowboy boots	two shots of bourbon
one beaded choker	one neck massage
one racy push-up bra	one hour with the car

one slinky kimono top	one late-night run for Chinese takeout
one condom	one mini Toblerone bar
one condom after midnight	one foot-long Toblerone bar
one long knit scarf	one waiting in long line at bar for drinks
one pair of dark sunglasses	one driving by his house incognito
one pair of Ugg boots	one shoveling car out of driveway
one cashmere twin set	one double date with her crush's evil twin
one sequined top on a weeknight	one going along on a bad date with her
one sequined top on a weekend	one going on a really bad date in place of her
one pair of favorite jeans	one-way ride to airport
one pair of favorite jeans for long holiday weekend	round-trip ride to airport with door-to-door service
one pair of knee-high boots	one letting her choose the movie rental
one pair of thigh-high boots	one letting her choose the movie rental and ice cream flavor
one leather jacket	one calling in sick for her
one wedding gown	three of her unopened wedding gifts

Bad Girl Swap Meets

It's true. The more you share with friends, the more you want it—bad. Do you find yourself waking up in the morning craving a strong swap? Has swapping started to affect your relationships? Are you addicted to the rush of bartering? Congratulations! You're a swapaholic! Don't stop now; you're just beginning to experience the highs of sharing with friends. (Pssst: If it were a bad thing, there would be a twelve-step program by now.) When you're a swapaholic, it's important to surround yourself with other swapaholics and do it as often as you can!

Swap Threads

This brilliant wardrobe solution lets bad girls pool their resources to purchase high-ticket items that they normally couldn't afford. The next time you're boutique hopping and see a ridiculously overpriced designer dress or jacket that you'd normally pass up, get a friend to co-purchase it with you and then arrange for shared custody. You get them on weekends and holidays while she acts as legal guardian during the week.

Swap Compliments

Even the baddest girls require the occasional ego stroke. That's why it's every bad girl's duty and honor to spread the love—every day, in lots of little ways. Compliment swapping is a two-way street: you've gotta give love to get it, which requires passing on the love baton. When you notice something special or new about one of your baddies, don't keep it to yourself—share it, for bad girl's sake! Take the time to point out her fab new highlights, that great shade of lipstick, her unique and original driving skills. And don't just drop it into conversation non-

time to end a relationship when you have to schedule sex dates and you

chalantly, make it an event. Dim the lights, ply her with soft music and hard drinks, then look deeply into her eyes and whisper the compliment with seductive sincerity and sinful sultriness, "I want you to know that I really, really like what you're doing with your bangs these days."

Swap Dates

You've got sushi at eight with Steve. She's got cocktails at nine with Dave. She loves raw fish. You love martinis. You're both a little bored. Switcheroo! There's really no need to call ahead to alert Steve or Dave. Just exchange crucial date details and show up with a devious smile and a confident attitude.

Swap Friends

Sick of going to the same parties, hearing the same stories, and having the same conversations over and over? Swaperoo! Throw a cocktail party at your place and invite all of the people on your friend's/sister's/roommate's speed dial rather than your own. Hand over your Rolodex

---

Giving and Getting Some TLC . . .

How can you be sure you get as many compliments as you give? Make a TLC (Tell Last Compliment) agreement with all you friends. The next time you hear a juicy, sweet compliment about a friend, remember it. The next time you see her, flaunt it in a sing-song voice—"I've got some TLC for you." Desperate to cash in, she'll do her duty—dishing up a yummy compliment about you first (real or imaginary). Once you are basking in the glow of your compliment, then you can proceed to give her some TLC. It's feel-good fun for all!

---

don't even have kids. You know it's time to start a relationship when you

or Palm Pilot and let her do the same. Then compare naughty notes and dishy details.

Swap Dirt

Think of this as a glorious gossip round-robin. If you don't have a long list of dirty laundry to air, don't show up. Once the group is gathered, the hostess kicks off the mud slinging with a round of cocktails and a juicy dollop of gossip. Next, the person to her left must offer up something equally trashy or titillating. And so on. If your turn comes and you don't have any dirt to dish, you must exit the party. Only the most diehard gossip hounds survive.

Swap Families

Are you tired of going home for the holidays? Are you sick of dealing with the same boring buried resentments, the predictable passive-aggressive prodding, the dull dining-room meltdowns year after year? If spending time with your family around the holidays is as much fun as finding parking at the mall on Christmas eve, then just swap families! Find a fearless friend who's dreading the holidays at home as much as you are and trade holiday travel plans. All you need to do is purchase a plane ticket to her house, hop in a cab, and show up at the front door with a suitcase full of gifts for your faux family. They'll be so thrown off by the surprise that they'll either be on their best behavior or forget their techniques for turning the holidays into hell. Either way, you and your friend might actually enjoy yourselves! If not, at least you'll be amused and entertained by your new family's dysfunction. And hey, maybe next year your real family won't seem so bad.

wake up every morning spooning your body pillow. You know it's time to end

The Bad Girl Jean Pool

It's survival of the fashion fittest. Are you in or out of it? Get your posse together for an evening of jean-etic testing and form your own DNA (Denim Now Association).

Each bad girl is invited to bring a few pairs of her most delicious denim. Be sure to include a diverse range of bootyful-sized girls, styles, and washes. Upon arrival, every pair of jeans is numbered and tagged for future tracking in the wild life. (Use an indelible Sharpie inside the waistband.) Then all jean pool members try on all the jeans to see which ones fit and can be comfortably shared. All jeans are then catalogued in a database (computer file or recipe file will do) and maintained by your most responsible baddie. You and all your bad girl friends get to draw from the DNA pool, sharing the love and style.

Jean Pool Rules

1. To get a pair, you have to give a pair.

2. Jeans must be returned clean and smelling fresh.

3. Jeans must be returned with a note in the pocket detailing the delicious mischief and bad-ventures that occurred while wearing them.

Every few months, get your DNA members together for a Bad Girl Jean Pool party. It's the perfect way to introduce new styles of denim, celebrate your friendship, and read aloud the best and the baddest notes!

Note to Self: Collect more data for "playing the field" study.

The Baddy System

Based on the buddy system where people are paired up for mutual safety and assistance, the Baddy System is designed to provide bad girls with a roster of baddies who can watch their backs and cover their booties when the going gets tough. Be sure to have one each of the following baddies in tow wherever you go.

The Baddy	**The Booty Coverage**
The Designated Drinker 	Spikes the party energy with her 100-proof personality, getting the dance floor grooving and ensuring a good time wherever you go.
The Designated Thinker	Keeps a clear head and does the thinking for your posse when the rest of you can't.
The Designated Shrinker	Holds impromptu therapy sessions when you're in need of an instant anti-anxiety cure.
The Designated Stinker	Plays the bad cop—telling rude waiters, creepy crawlers, and hangers-on where to get off.
The Pay Pal	Corporate tycoon or trust-fund babe who doesn't mind sharing the wealth and picking up the tab when you're tapped out.
The Gay Pal	The hot lesbian friend who makes them wonder if she's date or bait. Either way, the guys are swarming—they either think you're both

a relationship when you start flirting with other people at church. You know

	single or dream they might stand a chance of witnessing hot! lesbian! sex!
The Guy Pal	Metrosexual guy who balances estrogen levels and brings in style, fashion, and hot single extras when needed.
The Bi Pal	Rides both sides of the fence, supplying the posse with classified information and delicious dating tips from both camps.
The Social Activist	Committed to upholding the ideals of the bad girl posse—lobbying for radical plans and staging protests if anyone tries to bag out.

Friend Shui

Every bad girl dynasty should know and respect the powers of Friend Shui (pronounced *frend schway*)—the ancient Chinese art of positioning bad girls in the optimal locations to showcase their sassiest assets and keep their bad girl energy swirling in positive directions. When you achieve Friend Shui, you'll know it—every bad girl in your swirl will be feeling aligned, looking divine, and having a fabulous time.

To get your posse's She (bad girl life force) to vibrate in perfect harmony, you must identify and harness each baddy's unique physical and mental energy and then balance it all out using a few key principles.

Choosing Your Power Positions

Where do you stand with your power posse? Whether you're striking a pose at the bar, strutting into the party, or choosing the right booth at a restaurant or club, it's all about creating a bootyful balance and fab flow of energy.

Round lines **balance** hard edges, so be sure your posse consists of equal parts gentle, curvaceous creatures and edgy, angular types for maximum yin-yang balance. However, if your group's energy seems to be getting snagged on a friend with overly jagged points or a chronically sharp tongue, feel free to replace her with a smoother, softer someone or, better yet, try adding a funky new shape, style, or color that enhances the group love flow.

Avoid extreme **shape discrepancies**—if you've got a bodacious butt, avoid exiting a party beside a waif with mini-buns. If you're a perky A cup, don't go chest to chest with your double-D friend. Always position yourself beside like-shaped baddies for guaranteed glow and optimal social flow.

Mirrors are very important in Friend Shui. In a bar or restaurant, be sure to choose a booth across from a mirror so that you can always see which hotties are coming and going, discreetly spy on your various crushes, make two-way eye contact, and monitor whose lipstick needs to be reapplied.

If you feel your group **She** getting stuck, hang a crystal from the rearview mirror or congregate beneath a disco ball—the refraction of light will break up the blocked energy and get the group grooving.

button and haven't been to the movies for a week. You know it's time to end a

Clutter also **blocks** She, so if you've got a deadbeat bad girl or a downbeat good girl in tow, set her free at the next stop, and feel the She energy flow.

Balancing Yin & Yang

Yin and yang are two opposite yet equal extremes that brilliantly balance each other and keep the bad girl world swirling round. Yin girls tend to be the quieter types who store their energy and keep things calm. Yang girls are all about burning the essential oils and expending energy, keeping things spicy hot. But of course, there's a little bit of yin in every yang and vice versa.

Yin girls are . . .	Yang girls are . . .
big thinkers	big talkers
slow and steady	fast and ready
patient and caring	flagrant and daring
waiting for Mr. Right	dating Mr. Right Now
skilled conversationalists	skilled contortionists
designated drivers	designated dancers
under the radar	over the top
dressed accordingly	dressed scantily
off to bed early	off the hook early

relationship when you find a popcorn kernel in your belly button and haven't been

Friender Benders

When you're living in the fast lane on the bad girl free-way, you may occasionally find yourself in a nasty little friender bender. These communication collisions aren't that serious but need to be dealt with quickly, responsi-bly, and humorously to maintain your friendship with bad girl style.

After a typical friender bender, most girls act like every-thing is fine and just keep on cruising. They don't want a conflict, so they don't stop to acknowledge or assess the damage to their friendship. This inevitably leads to a (communication and/or nervous) breakdown down the road. Fortunately, bad girls aren't like most girls! We don't ignore the clash, we explore it, find the fun in it, vent our feelings, and move on.

But when a serious friender bender can't be resolved and laughed about over coffee, cocktails, a long walk, or an arm wrestle, then it's time to try one or more of the following Auto Therapies.

to the movies for a week. You know it's time to start a relationship when

Auto Therapies: Fun Ways to Clear the Air & Get On With It

Leaving your anger in the dust and moving forward with a grudge-free friendship can be tricky. That's when it's time to hit the road, reconnect to your bad girl roots, and take your relationship out for some intensive auto-neurotic therapy. Just check your inhibitions and rational adult behavior in the trunk, take your rage out of neutral, and floor it! Here are just a few fun, feel-good ways to add vice and blow out your mutual frustrations.

The Horn Hank-Off

Sometimes words just aren't enough. Let your horn do the talking. Meet in an empty parking lot, pull up fender to fender, and start to lay on your respective car horns. Communicate through a series of long wailing honks, short hysterical beeps, or an abstract improvisational horn symphony that expresses your emotions in a creative way. Rev your engines insanely for emphasis. Be sure that your inhibitions are off and your emergency brake is on!

you seriously think about getting a second cat. You know it's time to end a

The Merge & Purge

Jump in the car, head for the nearest on-ramp, merge into high-speed traffic, crank the music up, roll the windows down, and let each other have it in a simultaneous verbal merge and purge—unleashing all of your repressed anger at the tops of your lungs. The loud roar of your engine combined with your frenzied raging, the whizzing energy of the highway, wind whipping in your faces, and music blaring will all culminate in a glorious release of your pent-up emotions. When you start to run out of gas, look for an exit. You'll both feel refreshed and relieved and may even feel the urge to keep driving toward your next bad-venture.

The Merge and Purge is also a very effective rage releaser for one. As you drive, just scream at the top of your lungs, venting about whatever and whoever is making you crazy. Of course nearby motorists will think you are crazy—but who cares? They'll all back off and give you the right of way!

The "Can You Hear Me NOW?"

Bad communication can always be blamed on—and celebrated with—bad cell phone reception. Wait until you're both on the road and then call her cell from your cell. As you wait in traffic or maneuver through the city, start to lay into her. She can pretend not to hear you—"Sorry, what was that? You're breaking up." Or, she can start to fight back, at which point you have the option to feign bad reception and hang up—"Sorry, I'm going into a tunnel. Can't hear you." Continue to call each other back, repeating the exercise until you feel comfortable blaming the whole conflict on bad cell phone reception.

relationship when he gets more excited seeing his dog than you. You know it's

The Nervous Breakdown Lane

Take your conflict to the road and, just as you broach the subject of your dispute and feel your emotions rise, put on your hazards, pull over and into the breakdown lane, and surrender to a hysterical breakdown—sniffling, sobbing, and laughing simultaneously until you're both emotionally drained and puffy-eyed. If a cop or a good Samaritan pulls over to help you, ask for a box of tissues and an objective opinion.

The Car Wash Spout-Off

A drive-through car wash is the perfect place to clean your car and clear up your conflict in a matter of minutes—it's a safe, controlled environment designed to wash away the everyday buildup of crud in a dark, private chamber. As your car is doused in suds and sloshed over by those big black caterpillar things, let your feelings flow. Make a pact that by the time your car rolls off the rails, your foaming rage will be washed away and your friendship will feel shiny and new—and ready to road trip.

time to start a relationship when you get seven different wedding invitations in

No Wheels? No Problem!

Here are a few powerful pedestrian ways for you and your bad-versary to release your rage via nonverbal, physically creative activities.

Hit the Driving Range

Grab a bucket of balls and get whacking! It's amazing how much pent-up tension and anger can be released as you perfect your swing. By the time the bucket is empty, you'll be feeling back on par and ready to share a couple of Bloody Marys and BLTs at the clubhouse!

Find a Real Punching Bag

Instead of using each other as human punching bags, sign up for a boxing class at your local gym or YMCA. Strap on some gloves and bite hard on a mouth guard to prevent unnecessary small talk, then jab your resentment away. If that sounds too hardcore, then buy an inflatable punching clown and form a punch line!

Stomp the Madness

Drive to the nearest winery and ask if you can participate in a good old-fashioned wine stomping. Hop in the vat with your bad-versary and mash the living hell out of those grapes, splattering blood-red grape juice all over

the mail the same day. You know it's time to end a relationship when you make

each other. If you can't get to a winery, fill the bathtub with jumbo bubble wrap, add some grape juice for a dash of splash, then stomp the madness away. Once your frustrations have been stomped out and the grapes are properly smashed, the two of you can proceed to do the same over a nice bottle of Merlot.

Play Ball

Back in elementary school days, you didn't resolve conflicts over lattes, you hit the playground for a primal game of dodge ball. It's survival of the fittest—and it still feels great! Find an empty parking lot, draw an imaginary line, and start whipping one of those old, red rubber balls at each other. Throw for your life and scream like a fourth-grader. Once you're both covered in welts, call a truce and spend the rest of the afternoon nursing your wounds and reliving the best shots over double lattes.

a list of what you might inherit if he dies. You know it's time to start a relationship

Ms. Communication Says . . .

Life is full of conflict—and that's what makes it so interesting! The way you handle (or don't handle) your everyday scuffles and scandals affects how you feel about yourself, your friends, and your relationships—and how other people feel about you. Is your style of conflict resolution working for you or against you? Are you trying for closure with a friend but secretly targeting entrapment?

Let Ms. Communication, the unofficial expert on bad communication and conflict resolution, comment on what you're doing right, what you're doing wrong, and how to make it all feel badder.

Your resolution style: **Repress & Resent**

What you do: When someone or something pisses you off, you say nothing and then just smile quietly and carry a big grudge.

What it does to you: All of your anger and frustration implodes, leading to headaches, indigestion, ulcers, and unsightly blemishes.

What it does for your relationship: Adds a subtle yet palpable strain due to lack of honesty and festering resentment.

Ms. Communication says: Holding on to all that anger takes so much more energy than just letting it go. If you don't have anything nice to say, say it anyway! People will still like you. In fact, everyone—including you—will like and respect you even more. And, by the way, your skin will glow.

Your resolution style: **Public Verbal Stoning**

What you do: When crossed, you strike like a coiled cobra, spitting and spewing lethal, venomous words in front of friends, family, and the maitre d'.

What it does to you: Makes you feel vindicated and vivacious! But when she gets everyone's sympathy vote and you get voted most likely to be "a verbally abusive bitch who needs need serious anger management," then you realize you've not only lost your self-control, you've lost your personal power.

What it does for your relationship: Keeps it honest, but keeps her (and everyone else) from trusting you, liking you, and feeling safe around you.

Ms. Communication says: Easy, killer. It's great that you're comfortable expressing yourself and confronting a problem, but don't do it in front of a crowd. It only makes her feel like a jerk and you look like one. P.S. Projectile verbal vomiting is not communicating. If you think it is, get therapy and a punching bag.

Your resolution style: **Private Verbal Stoning**

What you do: Act super nice until you get her alone and then let her have it, holding nothing back.

What it does to you: Makes you feel ten pounds lighter and ten times meaner than you meant to be.

What it does for your relationship: Makes her fear and avoid you.

Ms. Communication says: Expressing yourself is good, but the way you're doing it is not. Just because you confront someone about a problem doesn't mean you have to be confrontational. Speak the truth from your heart and save the Mommy Dearest act for drama club.

when you both agree that casual sex is okay on casual Fridays. You know it's time

Your resolution style: **The Silent Mistreatment**

What you do: Clam up and ice her out. Give her nothing but cold looks and the cold shoulder until she finally asks what's wrong. At which point you say, "Nothing. Why do you ask?"

What it does to you: Makes you feel smugly (and falsely) in control while you seethe with anger—at her for playing dumb and at yourself for playing games.

What it does for your relationship: Turns it into a stupid game of rat and mouse—she's chasing you for approval and you're coyly withholding the stinky cheese.

Ms. Communication says: You're longing for someone to notice that you're in pain but actually prolonging your pain instead. This is a horrific mismanagement of time and energy. Quit punishing her for doing you wrong and punishing yourself in the process. Now *that's* miscommunication.

Your resolution style: **Passive-Regressive**

What you do: When your friend pisses you off, you react like a bratty child, stomping your feet or holding your hands over your ears and singing loudly to block out her explanation and apology.

What it does to you: Makes you look and feel like an immature brat.

What it does for your relationship: Nothing. She feels like the substitute teacher in your special ed. class.

Ms. Communication says: Grow up and learn the ABCs of clear communication before your friends start leaving you at home with a baby-sitter.

to start a relationship when your vibrator breaks from lack of use. You know it's

Your resolution style: **Conference Staller**

What you do: With dramatic diva flair, immediately ask to see her in the nearest ladies' room stall where you talk it out in your own private quarters, taking turns holding each other's purse while the other squats and pees.

What it does to you: Relieves you of your pent-up anger so you can enjoy the night with a clear conscience and empty bladder.

What it does for your relationship: Adds immediacy to your conflict resolution and intimacy to your friendship.

Miss Communication says: Brilliant! Friends who squat and pee together stay with glee together. Just be sure to flush all your resentments down the drain and wash your hands of guilt before you go.

Your resolution style: **The Oprah**

What you do: Sit her down on your big, cushy couch and sincerely ask why she behaved the way she did. Then calmly tell her how her actions made you feel. Then ask her how that makes her feel. Then weep and go to a commercial break.

What it does to you: Helps you process your feelings in a healthy way.

What it does for your relationship: Gives you an excuse to be couch potatoes at 4:00 in the afternoon or 4:00 in the morning.

Miss Communication says: Brava! What channel was that on? Damn, I should've TiVo-ed it.

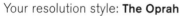

Bad Girl Boundaries: Saying No without Saying No

Even the closest friendships need boundaries. Some stuff you just don't feel like sharing and some days you just don't feel like explaining why. But how do you give your boundary-blind friend the hint without having to play the heavy? It's all in the twist action.

She asks:

Would it be weird for you if I dated your brother?

Can I borrow your lipstick?

Can you baby-sit Emma?

Can I borrow your toothbrush?

You say:

No! It would be so nice of you. With his new medication, he's so much better. You can hardly tell he's . . . you know.

Sure! My cold sore is pretty much gone. Does this spot look funny to you?

I'd be honored. And I really appreciate your not holding that whole baby-shaking thing against me. That was so sensationalized! Really, I love kids!

Of course—it's my favorite one. I've had it since, like, third grade.

Can I stay at your place for a while?

Absolutely! I've got an air mattress. You're cool with cockroaches, right? They're not that big. And they only come out at night.

Can I borrow your hairbrush?

No prob! Those little white things aren't alive anymore. So it's not contagious. At least that's what I read on the Internet.

Can I borrow that shirt?

Please do! Let me just give it a whiff to make sure the dry cleaner got the garlic-infused BO smell out.

Is it cool if I date your ex?

Go for it! I'm just happy that you're not hung up on size. Like it really matters!

Can I borrow your car?

Sure thing! The accelerator kind of sticks every now and then. All you have to do is pop the clutch really fast and then hit the brakes until it unsticks. The keys are in my purse!

Homeland Security

Speaking of personal threats and invasions of space, we've all experienced an extended visit from those pesky houseguests who can't get enough of your pull-out sofa, free food, liquor cabinet, DVD collection—and can't take a hint. If you're having trouble getting your guests to ship out, here are some not-so-subtle hints that you might want to drop.

* Replace the down in their pillows with popcorn and damp dog hair.

* Turn off plumbing and electricity (and heat if it's winter).

* Replace all breakfast cereals with foam packing peanuts.

* Needlepoint a quaint sign to hang in kitchen with a bad adage that reads, "Houseguests are like fish. After three days, they stink and drive me to drink."

* Hide all the towels and tell them you believe in air drying. It's for the environment, stupid.

* When they head into the bathroom for a long, steamy shower, turn on the sprinklers, start a load of laundry, and run the dishwasher.

* Get into a screaming fit with your boyfriend, husband, or pet and then flee the house in fake tears. Go to a movie.

* Hire professional movers to start packing up everything in the house, starting with the pull-out sofa.

together for fun. You know it's time to start a relationship when the only one

* Set up a string of back-to-back consultations with exterminators and then ask your guest to answer the door while you run a few errands.

* Crank-call your house from a pay phone and breathe heavily into the mouthpiece, whispering "I know where you live. I'm coming to get you."

* Tell your sister you'll watch her four kids and then let them run wild, suggesting that they play dress-up with the clothes in that pretty suitcase in the corner.

* Frequently forget to flush the toilet.

* Replace toothpaste in guest bathroom with Ben-Gay.

* Buy a ferret and potty train it in your guestroom.

* Walk around with a stick of burning incense. When they ask what you're doing, say, "Trying to rid this evil dwelling of satanic spirits. Can you feel the devil's presence? I can."

* Eat bean burritos every day for lunch and develop a little gas problem. Fart loudly while you watch TV beside them on the couch. Act like you don't notice.

* Ask them to help you move the furniture around, starting with the 200-pound armoire. Be indecisive and try it in a lot of different places.

stealing the covers at night is your dog. You know it's time to end a relationship

Bad Houseguest Etiquette

Managing houseguests is one thing. Being the houseguest is another. Here's a quick guide on how to behave if you want to be invited back.

Houseguest Do's and Don'ts

Do bring a nice bottle of wine. **Don't** insist that they open it immediately and then proceed to polish it off yourself.

Do the dishes. **Don't** do her roommate.

Do take out the trash. **Don't** dig through the trash and then comment on your findings. ("A home pregnancy test! I had no idea you were trying to get knocked up!")

Do fold up the sofa bed each morning. **Don't** leave pillows, blankets, dirty undies, and your slinky negligee strewn all over the living room.

Do tidy up around the house. **Don't** vacuum wearing only your leopard-print thong.

Do help fold their laundry. **Don't** comment on their underwear. ("Jeez, Jerry. Nice skid marks!")

Do call ahead. **Don't** call all of your friends in Eastern Europe.

when your Labrador is smarter than he is. You know it's time to start a relationship

Do offer to make a nice candlelit dinner for your hosts. **Don't** start a grease fire and burn down their house.

Do fluff the sofa pillows. **Don't** offer to fluff the pizza delivery boy in lieu of a tip.

Do try to bond with their children. **Don't** have a long talk with little Billy about where babies come from.

Do mingle with their friends. **Don't** invite one of their friends to stay over with you and get personal on the pull-out sofa.

Do offer to pick up a new release at Blockbuster. **Don't** comment on the hidden porn stash under the sofa.

Do feel free to use your electric toothbrush before bed. **Don't** feel free to use your vibrator before bed.

when you can't remember how to use a condom. You know it's time to end a

Big Love

Getting Personal with Your Romantic Co-Star

If your search for big love is a big problem, then you're probably taking it way too seriously. Big love should be big fun! Like going to the movies. Think about it—what is a romantic relationship really? It's the ultimate form of entertainment! So treat it that way and be as relaxed about choosing a date as you are about choosing a movie on a date.

It's simple. Just ask yourself what kind of relationship you're in the mood for. A romantic comedy? A tear-jerker? An epic saga? A foreign film? A buddy movie? An action adventure? Are you craving a PG-13 animated cartoon? Or something rated R, X, or XXX? Don't analyze it too much, don't judge yourself, and don't worry what anyone else will think. If it sounds fun, give it a try. Hey, it's just two hours of your relationship life.

Once you figure out what type of relationship movie you want, then you'll know if the person you're dating (or hoping to date) is your ideal romantic co-star. So turn off your cell phone, your emotional neediness, and your expectations of perfection. Then sit back, relax, pass the popcorn, and enjoy the relationship show.

Note to Self: Must visit relationship multiplex this weekend.

relationship when you don't even bother to fake orgasms. You know it's time to

What's with all the boring names? Boyfriend, girlfriend, husband, significant other, partner, mate, main squeeze, better half . . . Yawn! The first step to doing it baddy style with your big love is choosing the right love handle. The nickname you choose should get your motor running, put a smile on your face, and reflect the unique qualities of your relationship.

It's time to graduate from old school to bold school!

Old School Name	Bold School Name
Better Half	Badder Half
Main Squeeze	Main Tease
Boyfriend	Oh, Boy! Friend
Partner	Partner in Sublime Crime
Significant Other	Significant Bother
Girlfriend	Suck Buddy (*Eeeew!*)
Husband	Hoseman
Life Mate	Playmate
Lover	Big Lover

Badder yet, try a few of these on for size or create your own sexy love handles!

May I introduce you to my . . .

Beddy Buddy	Secret Agent of Love
Screamin' We-We	Under the Covers Agent
Pleasure Power Tool	Funny Boner
Main Attraction	Sweet Honey Love Muffin
Cowboy Toy	Romantic Co-Star

Note to Self: Must dress better in personal fantasies!

Dating Tip: Never wear inexpensive lipstick on a hot date. It tastes cheap! And, honey, you may be easy but you are not cheap.

start a relationship when you watch *Pretty Woman* and seriously wonder if

Dream Dating Bad Libs

On the perfect first date, we'll . . .

flirt shamelessly.

endure awkward silences with nervous laughter.

lock eyes by candlelight.

lock lips in the soft, glowing moonlight.

share embarrassing stories from our childhood.

hold hands all the way home.

watch shooting stars.

On the perfect fifth date, we'll . . .

do it shamelessly.

endure awkward roommates with nervous laughter.

lock the bedroom door.

lock lips in the soft glow of a Power Puff Girls nightlight.

share embarrassing stories from our sex lives.

hold each other all night long.

watch the sun rise.

On the perfect thirty-fifth date, we'll . . .

eat shamelessly.

endure awkward bodily emissions with nervous laughter.

lock the bathroom door.

lock lips in the soft glow of cable TV.

share embarrassing stories from our credit reports.

hold the remote all night long.

watch our soft bellies rise.

How Bad Is Your Relationship?

1. When he walks in the room, I feel _____.
A. dirty and my guilt races
B. dizzy and my heart races
C. irresistible and my imagination races

2. My recurring relationship nightmare is _____.
A. being left at the altar
B. being left at the altar naked
C. being the last one picked for naked Ultimate Frisbee

3. On my third date, the goodnight kiss _____.
A. never happened
B. tasted like garlic
C. never ended

4. The raciest thing I do in bed requires_____.
A. two double A batteries
B. two double D cup cakes
C. two Doublemint twins

5. Our typical relationship conflict resolution requires _____.
A. heavy conversation
B. heavy drinking
C. heavy petting

6. On a blind date I have been known to _____.
A. get into a polite debate about the Middle East
B. get hammered and get naked
C. get stuck in the bathroom window trying to escape

7. I know we need couples therapy when we _____.
A. can't get through dinner without fighting
B. can't get through sex without fighting
C. can't get through sex without breaking for dinner

(A Quiz)

8. Flirting outside of my relationship is a sign of _____.

A. very bad manners
B. very good things to come
C. a very confident, hot, and healthy bad girl

9. In my relationship future, I see _____.

A. a husband, two kids, and a luxury SUV
B. an agent, a lawyer, and a corporation with my name on it
C. all of the above and a sexy cabana boy cleaning my pantyliner-shaped pool

10. On a typical romantic weekend getaway, I _____.

A. burn his shirt while ironing
B. burn rubber in the backseat
C. burn up the phone lines trying to post bail

11. The last time I got really bad in bed, I secretly wanted _____.

A. Vaseline and a body double
B. Vicodin and a double martini
C. a video camera and a do-over

12. I only want to see my evil ex _____.

A. happily married with a carload of screaming kids
B. crawling back to beg for my forgiveness
C. in an itsy-bitsy Speedo on a reality TV show

13. When you hear "un-cut," you think of _____.

A. a diamond
B. the *David*
C. the *South Park* movie

RESULTS: Count the C's
Your Relationship Is
Legally Bland: 0–4
Legally Bad: 5–9
Regally Bad: 10 or more

Man Overboard!

Bad girls, beware when dating one of these over-the-top characters. They may have sexy, curb appeal, but they're so full of themselves they will drive you crazy.

George Loony: so handsome and charismatic you ignore the fact that he's nuts

Ben Affected: success has gone to his pretty little blow-dried head

Harrison Bored: strong and solid but painfully predictable

Bad Pit: thinks his muskiness is sexy, but it just stinks

Hugh Can't: charming and witty but in bed he's a pity

Poo Daddy: shamelessly worships his regal visits to the throne

Kevin I Need My Spacey: so commitment phobic, he makes you wonder

Alexander I'm So Great: he is on a life mission, and it is not you

Phlegminem: thinks he's so street and cool, hocks loogies to prove it

Jim Scary: needs so much attention that he's always in full-performance mode

Luke Starfucker: wimpy and short but so well connected he only dates actresses, models, and royalty

Throbbie Williams: such a sexy love machine that you can't see straight when you're near him—or see that he's working every curve in the room

prostitution is the best way to meet the man of your dreams. You know it's time to

The Bad Girl's Vibe Guide

On your first few dates, pay attention to the details and trust your gut vibe! He is who he is—not the guy you think he could be after you get the chance to fix him. The morning after your first few dates, review this list:

__ BAD BOY. He's funny, confident, genuine, and feeling his mojo. And he loves to inspire delicious mischief.

__ MAD BOY. He's prone to explosive verbal and/or physical outbursts, followed by weepy apologies. Run for it before you need a restraining order!

__ SAD BOY. He's pathetic and/or depressed and the ideal relationship codependent. He may be sweet but he will bring you down!

__ HAD BOY. He's hot but he's been done by every girl you know. Pass the baton—you deserve fresh meat.

__ RAD BOY. He's cool, he's daring, he's fresh. He's not afraid to beat the rush, challenge the norm, or take an extreme position in any debate.

__ CAD BOY. He's a smooth operator but he doesn't even pretend to care about you or your feelings. You don't have time for this nasty narcissist!

__ GLAD BOY. He's fashionable, fun, smart, gossipy, and gay. Not a great full-service date but could become your new baddest friend.

Be honest! If you aren't, then you have no one to blame but yourself for getting sucked into an unhappy and/or unfulfilling relationship.

end two relationships when your boyfriend smells like your best friend's perfume.

Paving Over Your Relationship Potholes

With an active bad girl love style, mistakes can happen—and often last months or even years. But why beat yourself up about an embarrassing, humiliating, degrading, tragic relationship when you can beat it into a frothy story? A bad girl knows that once you've learned your relationship lesson, you should move on and never, ever repeat it—to anyone!

Good girls have regrets about past relationships—bad girls have good stories!

Your Relationship History

It was an embarrassing rebound.

The only good thing was the sex.

I needed to be the successful one.

Mostly, we did drunken booty calls.

We were both too depressed to break up.

Your Relationship Story

I really wanted to try something new and piss off my parents.

I was learning to stay out of my head and really be in my body.

I sponsored a troubled youth for six months.

I had free booty-call waiting.

It lasted longer than it should have, but our rhythms and energy were so in sync.

I slept with my professor all semester.

She was my yoga instructor.

He was so young and so horny.

I was afraid to be single and lonely.

I was afraid to be single and lonely
and I wanted help with the rent.

He was married and he still is.

I fell for a major drama queen.

It was totally sexless.

He was my ex-boyfriend's best friend.

We partied a lot together.

It started as a drunken hook-up.

He was much older and paid for everything.

He was gay!

One semester, I got straight A's in Human Sexuality.

She totally came on to me—you should have seen
her downward dog.

I was both the teacher and the student.

I was saving to buy a house so I wanted help
with the rent.

I was doing character research for my screenplay.

He died in a fiery crash.

I was stalked by a crazy slut.

We were really good buddies.

We had so much in common.

On the relationship highway, we got stuck in a
pothole and stalled.

We partied a lot together.

I was in a mentoring program.

We had a ton of fun together, but, in the end, he just
wasn't my type.

The Date Decoder

What he says:

I'm craving Indian food tonight.

I think we have some friends in common.

I'm a vegetarian.

Bring us your most expensive bottle of wine.

My mom is my best friend.

I was home-schooled.

My motorcycle is in the shop.

I couldn't get cash. My ATM card is, like, demagnetized or something.

What he means:

We're not hooking up tonight.

I'm also dating a friend of yours.

Don't expect me to go down on you.

I want to impress you and I know nothing about wine.

I have serious issues relating to women and am clueless about it.

I'm super smart and socially stunted.

If you saw my car, you'd never go out with me.

I'm broke.

Let's go back to your place.

Let's go back to my place.

I am currently exploring a variety of interesting career opportunities.

I have a really early meeting in the morning.

Want to see a picture of my dog?

Ditto.

My place is a dump and I don't have cable.

My roommate's away this weekend.

I don't have health insurance.

If this gets too emotionally intense, I'm going to bolt.

Want to see who I sleep with every night?

I love you, too.

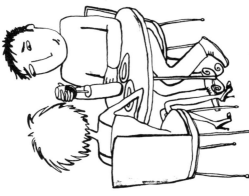

The Truth about Dogs and Men

The Dog	What He Thinks It Says	What It Really Says
Golden Retriever	I've got the original best dog ever.	I'm never original or clever.
Dachsund	I like cute, small wiener dogs.	I have a cute, small wiener.
German Shepherd	I am very disciplined.	Can I sniff your crotch?
Afghan Hound	I'm really high class.	I'm really high maintenance.
Coonhound	I'm a country boy.	My sister is also my wife.
Toy Poodle	Size doesn't matter.	I sure hope size doesn't matter to you.
Pit Bull	I'm gang-sta bad.	I'm a drug-dealing los-ah.
Rottweiler	My dog can kick your ass.	Would you whip my ass?

English Bulldog	I don't care about looks.
Great Dane	I like things BIG.
Bichon Frise	I'm *très* sophisticated.
Jack Russell Terrier	I'm spunky, smart, and very tenacious.
Dalmatian	I'm an off-duty fireman.
Collie	I'm a safe, reliable guy.
Mutt	I'm easygoing and unpretentious.
Doberman Pinscher	I'm in charge.

	I'm a slob, too.
	I couldn't afford a horse.
	I'm way confused about my sexuality.
	I've got A.D.D.
	My dog's name is Spot.
	Will you and Lassie save me?
	I'm easygoing and unpretentious.
	I like it ruff, ruff!

Is It a Match?

How do you know if the heat you feel on a date is for real? Check this list. Be honest with yourself. If you're not, you're playing with fire and will eventually get burned.

Combustible Match: immediate, explosive, uncontrollable sex, er, rather, attraction

Safety Match: your no-risk, no-sizzle fallback guy

Smoking Match: the heat and smell lingers long after the date

Lit Match: only works when you're both drunk

Zippo Lighter: flashy on the outside but no sparks on the inside

Wet Match: feels oh-so-good and gets your juices flowing

Broken Match: could've worked but you snapped

Trick Match: the fire never goes out because only one of you is always paying

Disposable Lighter: you only use it because it's cheap and handy

Foot-Long Fireplace Match: ignites your fire and burns hot all night long

Note to Self: Why be engaged to one when you can be engaging to many?

You know it's time to start a relationship when you start thinking office memos

Your Personal MANdate Checklist

Before you set a MANtrap, make sure he's the kind of man you really want. After your first date, check this list. After your second date, double-check it.

__ MANtra: He's spiritual and calming.
__ MANipulative: He's sly and not to be trusted.
__ MANager: He's a bossy know-it-all.
__ MANologue: He talks nonstop about himself.
__ MANic: He's nuts.
__ MANgy: He's scruffy and needs a bath.
__ MANhandler: He treats you rough.
__ MANilla: He's brown and buff.
__ MANacle: He wants to shackle you to him.
__ MANkind: He's a genuine sweetie.
__ MANsion: He's got bucks and the house to prove it.
__ MANeuverer: He's way too smooth an operator.
__ MANnered: He's insecure and trying too hard.
__ MANopause: He's got to be at least fifty.
__ MANi-Pedi: His nails are better than yours.
__ MANna: He's a yummy godsend.
__ MAN-o-War: He's constantly picking fights.
__ MANifest Destiny: He thinks he's entitled to you.
__ MANdolin: He has a pear-shaped body.
__ MANservant: He wants to be your house boy.
__ MANhattan: He's very cosmopolitan.
__ MANpower: He's strong and confident.
__ MANnequin: He's a stiff and total phony.
__ MANure: He's full of shit.
__ MANage à Trois: He's so hot you want to share him with a good friend.

are really secret love letters. You know it's time to end a relationship when you

Relationship Flags

Early in a relationship, the signs are always there in the little things he says and does. But if you ignore them and snooze, you'll definitely lose. The question is, do you want to pay attention now or pay later? A self-respecting bad girl reads the signs and has the guts to take the next exit.

Red Flags: *obvious negatives*

If you ask about his relationship history, he screams, jumps up, and brings you his stash of action figures.

He has a photo of his guru on the back of the toilet.

He keeps lipstick in his medicine cabinet.

He kisses you the way he kisses his dog.

When he uses the word love, he's talking about his hair.

His healthiest long-term relationship is with his therapist(s).

He has a frequent shopper card from the Lusty Lady!

Green Flags: *obvious positives*

If you ask about his relationship history, he shakes his head and laughs at himself.

He has a *Mad* magazine and a *Fortune* on the back of his toilet.

He kisses you like he's gently eating a ripe peach.

He keeps Liquid Silk and condoms in the medicine cabinet.

When he uses the word love, he's talking about his friends.

His healthiest long-term relationship is with his father.

He has a frequent shopper card from REI.

Aubergine Flags: *obvious signs he's a vegetable*

If you ask about his relationship history, he looks at you with a blank stare.

He has white supremacy magazines on the back of his toilet.

He kisses you like Mr. Potato Head.
He keeps Crisco in his medicine cabinet.
When he uses the word love, he's talking about his truck.
His healthiest long-term relationship is with the little man
   in his pants.
He has a frequent shopper card from Guns R Us.

Pink Flags: *obvious signs he loves*
   (and respects) bad girls
If you ask about his relationship
   history, he just smiles and winks.

He has a *Bad Girl's Guide* on the back of his toilet.
He kisses you the way you imagine kissing yourself.
He keeps pantyliners and a felt pen in his medicine cabinet.
When he uses the word love, he's talking about your sense
   of humor.
His healthiest long-term relationship is with his inner wild.
He has a frequent shopper card from Condomania.

Drink Flags: *obvious signs he loves (and disrespects)*
   alcohol
If you ask about his relationship history, he can't remember.
He has a martini shaker and cocktail on the
   back of the toilet.
He kisses you like an ashtray.
He keeps airline-sized bottles of booze in his
   medicine cabinet.
When he uses the word love, he's talking about
   ibuprofen and a Bloody Mary.
His healthiest long-term relationship is with his
   beer belly.
He has a frequent shopper card from Annie's
   Bail Bonds.

The In-Bedded Reporter

It's looking very good if . . .

The first time you stay over at his place, you wake up and find a rose on the bedside table.

Foreplay involves frosting, whipped cream, and sprinkles.

He calls you when he says he will.

The second time you stay over at his place, he gives you a sexy, little nickname (and knows how to use it!).

He serves you breakfast in bed—and it's really yummy!

You both wake up at six a.m. because you're too excited to sleep.

His idea of pillow talk is telling you how much he loves your body and your brain.

No directions are required to reach your orgasmic destination together.

He scrubs the tub, then draws you a bubble bath—and joins you.

The morning after, he takes you to brunch and introduces you to his friends.

He can't stop smiling at you, touching you, or kissing your neck.

The third time you stay over at his place, he cleans out a sock drawer for you.

To show his fidelity, he gives you a bouquet of inflated colored condoms.

He buys the first toothbrush.

It's not looking good if . . .

He tries to seduce you with talk about his high-thread-count sheets.

The first time you stay over at his place, his dog sleeps with you.

He calls you by another girl's name.

His ex has forbidden him to have sex in front of the cat they used to share. And he complies.

He refuses to use a condom.

The second time you stay over, he asks you to pop the zit on his back.

He calls you by his pet's name.

Every time you bend over, he thinks it's an invitation to do it doggy style.

His idea of pillow talk is calling voicemail to check his cell phone messages.

He can't get it up without porn.

The third time you stay over, he falls asleep before you get into bed.

You're sleeping together, but he never introduces you to his friends.

He calls you Mom.

Note to Self: Kiss and tell? No. Kiss and sell? Yes!

get mad and your significant other doesn't even notice. You know it's time to start

The Truth about Underwear and Men

The Style	What He Thinks It Says	What It Really Says
Tighty whities	I am so normal.	I am so normal it hurts.
Droopy grays	I don't give a damn about clothes.	Oh damn! I should've gone commando.
Cotton boxers	I like my space.	I'm subject to chafe.
Plaid flannel	I'm a good-time frat boy.	My shorts stink.
Silk boxers	I'm rich.	I am bitch.
Joe Boxers	I'm so wild and wacky.	I hope my shorts will distract you while I dive under the covers.
Boxer briefs	I'm super hip.	My boy/girlfriend buys my underwear.
Monogrammed boxers	I'm old-money royalty.	I'm an ass.

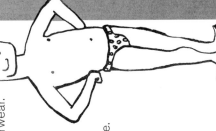

Jock strap	I'm athletic.	I'm pathetic and haven't done laundry in weeks.
Thong	I'm a slave to fashion.	Can I be your slave?
Freeballing	I'm too cool for underwear.	I'm too broke for underwear.
Animal-print banana hammock	Me Tarzan. You Jane.	Me Tarzan. Me insane.
Women's panties	I like to get kinky sometimes.	I'd like to borrow your pumps sometime.
Long johns	I'm always prepared.	I'm scared of shrinkage.

Can This Relationship Be Saved?

No. Face it. Some relationships simply do not deserve to live. They are unhealthy from the start and doomed to a life of pain and eternal suffering (yours!). They don't deserve a second, third, or fourth chance; they deserve a "Do Not Resuscitate" order—stat!

Signing a Bad Girl Power of Love

To keep you from heroic (and crazy) efforts to save a terminally ill relationship, you should sign over a Bad Girl Power of Love to a trusted clear-thinking friend. Choose someone who shares your relationship values and has the personal strength to pull the plug on your toxic love affair. This Bad Girl Power of Love document authorizes your friend to act on your behalf when you are not emotionally or mentally well. He or she must review your Relationship Living Will and Living Won't and then evaluate your relationship to see if you are living the relationship you wanted. If you are, then your relationship gets life support from you and your friends. If not, your friend makes the decision to pull the plug. And you've got to follow her advice—she's got your Bad Girl Power of Love.

a relationship when you keep an extra toothbrush at your place, just in case.

Relationship Rehab

Can—and should—this relationship be saved? When evaluating the condition of your rocky relationship, do not confuse . . .

* intimacy with inta-messy.

* a cute pain with acute pain.

* relationship heaven with a relationship haven.

* unconditional love with unconditional lust.

* mutual respect with mutual fund respect.

* a significant other with a significant bother.

* the big easy with the big sleazy.

* a commitment ceremony with a ceremony by committee.

* you feeling your best with him feeling your breast.

* a blissful marriage with a blissful mirage.

* tantric sex with tantrum sex.

Find a quiet time to write out your Relationship Living Will and Living Won't. These will help guide you through difficult twists and turns in any relationship. They become your reality check and balance. Be sure you're calm, sober, and thinking rationally, and then ask yourself what you will achieve and won't tolerate in a relationship. Here are two examples to inspire you. Feel free to modify to best suit the needs of your relationship life support. When you're satisfied, frame them or laminate them and use them as placemats.

You know it's time to end a relationship when you would rather go swimsuit

Relationship Living Will

I will take control of my relationship destiny.

I will have fun in every relationship!

I will pull the plug if I'm not getting enough support.

I will ask for what I need and know that I deserve to get it all.

I will trust my gut instinct in every situation.

I will love my butt and every other soft fleshy inch of my body!

I will stalk only as a last resort.

I will put fun in my dysfunctional family.

I will say no.

I will follow my heart, especially if it freaks out my parents.

I will be a strong and fearless communicator.

I will be a top.

I will make the world a badder place.

I will spritz the world with Baddy Sauce and shower it with love.

I will laugh at myself.

I will be irresistible.

Relationship Living Won't

I won't put up with abuse of any kind.

I won't be in a relationship unless I feel like an equal partner.

I won't kiss and tell too many people.

I won't be weak and wimpy and give my personal power away.

I won't fake an orgasm unless absolutely necessary.

I won't swallow—my pride, my bad girl spirit, or anything else that grosses me out!

shopping, 10 pounds overweight, than spend time with him. You know it's time to

I won't be anyone's doormat.

I won't act like a jealous lunatic.

I won't stay in a lousy relationship because I'm afraid to be alone.

I won't ever ask, "Do I look fat?"

I won't steal another girl's boyfriend unless she begs me to.

I won't wait to be asked.

I won't expect my boyfriend to act like a girlfriend.

I won't compare myself to his ex-girlfriends.

I won't get plastic surgery just to please a man.

I won't name our kids on the third date.

I won't feel guilty for going after what I want.

I won't have butt envy.

While you're at it, be sure to fill in your dream date details . . .

**My Living Will & My Living Won't
(personal dating commandments)**

I will never _____ on the first date.

I will never _____ on the second date.

I will always _____ on the third date.

I won't go on another date if _____.

If my date ever _____, I'm out of there.

If my date doesn't _____, I'm out of there.

I will always _____ my body.

I won't ever _____ my body.

I will never _____ someone else's body.

I will never drink _____ out of a _____.

start a relationship when you need a presentable date for your high school

Creative Ways to Break Up

Things to say . . .

It's not you, it's me. I deserve much, much better.

When I first met you, I thought I was someone else. And now that I know you better, I realize I am not who you want me to be or who I really could be. And I respect you too much to let you settle for that person.

I know it's just our third date but . . . Will you marry me? Say, yes! Oh, please, please say yes! If you do, I'll be your best friend and if you don't, I'll kill myself.

Let's go to couple's therapy.

Frankly, you can't afford me.

I'm sorry, but you remind me of my mother.

I really like you and want to keep dating. You should know I've got this little hormone imbalance that causes hair to grow all over my body. And I mean all over. So how about Saturday night?

I realize I can't date you anymore. I've met someone else. My inner bad girl!

Things to do . . .

Stash a box of pantyliners in his medicine cabinet.

Blow up photos of the two of you, frame them, and place in every room in your house. Hang one from your rearview mirror to seal the deal.

Flirt with his sister.

Tell his best friend that he is secretly in love with him.

Invite all your bad girl friends over to his place during Superbowl Sunday for a gabfest.

Call his mother every day.

Fake your death and move to another country.

reunion. You know it's time to end a relationship when you've been dating for

Things to Do with . . . Your Ex's Keys

* Make wind chimes for a sweet, tinkling, no-toilet-seat-up reminder of why he was all wrong for you

* Spray-paint pink, add earring hooks, and wear as fashionable earrings. You're *so* Janet Jackson!

* Pin to the breast of your jacket like medals of honor and wear with pride

* Add to your "not-so-charming ex" charm bracelet

* Throw into a fountain (ideally in Rome), make a wish for something much better, and do a little freedom dance

* Clean under your fingernails

* Pick dead bugs from the grille on your next road trip

* Hook to your nipple ring. You're *so* Janet Jackson!

* Attach a card with his name, home address, and cross street, then drop in a really scary neighborhood. Don't forget to list his electronics.

* Kindly return to your ex's lock and snap off

* Adhere to a page in your *Bad Girl's Scrappy Book* (Be sure to include all the hilarious relationship details!)

* Graciously present to his rebound woman in a grand public ceremony

* Decorate with a glitter pen and Super Glue to your bad girl tiara

six months and he still hasn't introduced you to his friends. You know it's time

Balancing Your Personal Emotional Budget

You do the math . . .

Personal Detail: He's a bit of a stoner.
+ **Personal Add:** You'll never have to make your own late-night Ramen again.
− **Personal Subtract:** He has trouble remembering your name, getting it up, and getting his unmotivated ass to the gym to lose his not-so-cute little gut that you get to watch jiggle when he sways to the Dead.

Personal Detail: He's an obsessive stalker.
+ **Personal Add:** You'll always feel loved and wanted.
− **Personal Subtract:** You'll always feel weird and watched.

Personal Detail: He wears more jewelry than you.
+ **Personal Add:** He appreciates the value of real diamonds.
− **Personal Subtract:** He's with the mob.

Personal Detail: His last girlfriend turned out to be a lesbian.
+ **Personal Add:** He probably gives great oral sex.
− **Personal Subtract:** He probably turns out to be gay.

Personal Detail: On special occasions, he wears a kilt.
+ **Personal Add:** You can share clothes.
− **Personal Subtract:** His legs are better than yours.

Personal Detail: He's a Buddhist.
+ **Personal Add:** He is selfless, especially in bed.
− **Personal Subtract:** You feel like a neurotic stress ball!

Personal Detail: His hobby is working on cars.
+ **Personal Add:** You'll never have to pay for a mechanic.
− **Personal Subtract:** You'll never see his hands clean.

to start a relationship when you become jealous of worms because they can mate

Personal Detail: He speaks only in song lyrics.
+ **Personal Add:** Finally, a good use for all those ridiculous lyrics taking up space in your wasted memory!
− **Personal Subtract:** He has nothing original to say.

Personal Detail: His man breasts are bigger than your breasts.
+ **Personal Add:** You'll never even be tempted to feel self-conscious about your body around his.
− **Personal Subtract:** You'll never even be tempted by his.

Personal Detail: He's much older and much richer than you.
+ **Personal Add:** Free stuff!
− **Personal Subtract:** What you have to touch to get it.

Bad Girl Gift Translator

If he gives you:	He wants:
flowers	to impress you
a teddy bear	to be your daddy
a poem	you to be his muse
a photo of himself with another girl	his face on a dart board
indigestion	cooking lessons
a kiss	you
attitude	to go home alone
a book	to be the teacher's pet
sweet nothings	to make out
a home-burned CD	you to think about him and get your groove on
expensive jewelry	you to forgive him
the giggles	to be your romantic comedy co-star
an STD	you to kill him

with themselves. You know it's time to end a relationship when he starts going

Promoting Your Single Self

Whether you're looking for a new friend, a new boyfriend, or a new shopping partner, be creative! A bad girl never limits herself to the usual suspects or the usual methods of attracting them—and she always enjoys the thrill of the hunt. Think big, think bold, think badvertising!

(Room)Mate Wanted Tear-Off Sign

What you need: Lots of hot pink paper, tape, thumb tacks, a catchy headline

> **Bad Girl Seeks Good Times!**
> Looking for:
> Great guy with room for new views
> Sunny disposition
> Cozy hugs and kisses
> Long-term parking
> Sense of humor a plus
> No drug users or depressed losers, please

What you do: Write a head-turning Mate Wanted sign, include your bad girl alias and a phone number twelve times at the bottom of the page, then cut for easy tearing. Post all over town.

Mount a Political Campaign

What you need: A vision of your relationship future, a winning slogan that's means something to someone

> **Join Joanne!** A new generation of booty calls
> **Candidate Me!** Finally, a cause your parents will protest
> **Demo This Democracy!** Naked-ization without representation

out with his friends more than you. You know it's time to start a relationship when

Your Future Is Wow! A date with a Bad Girl is a vote for fun

What you do: Gather a group of volunteers who are committed to your cause (you!).

Make signs, flyers, and buttons with your name and slogan.

Canvas your neighborhood cafes, bars, churches, and supermarkets, spreading the word about what you can offer the people.

Feel free to put together an "I'd date (your name here)" petition and collect names, numbers, and signatures of people who think you're hot.

Personal PowerPoint Presentation

What you need: A computer, clear organization of your best-selling points, a strong conclusion

What you do: Create an irresistible personal PowerPoint presentation, then e-mail it to everyone! A compelling title will pique the viewer's interest.

Sample title page: Who *Doesn't* Want to Date Carol?

Focus on your strengths:

Carol is super fun!

* on the dance floor
* on the phone

(Photos help illustrate your point and hold the viewer's attention!)

you pee with all doors wide open so you can hear the kitchen radio. You know

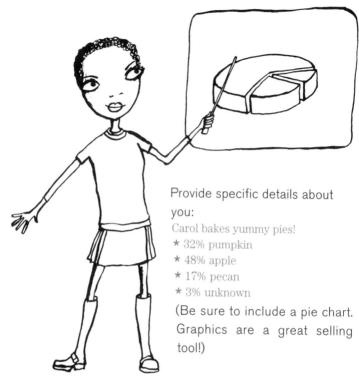

Provide specific details about you:

Carol bakes yummy pies!

* 32% pumpkin
* 48% apple
* 17% pecan
* 3% unknown

(Be sure to include a pie chart. Graphics are a great selling tool!)

Put a positive spin on everything:

Carol is never bitter about:

* being single (again!).
* her mean, dumb-ass boss (loser!).
* never making cheerleader (it was totally rigged!).

End with a strong and specific conclusion:

Next Steps:

* E-mail Carol a response and a photo right now.
* Include age, zodiac sign, height, weight, and shoe size.
* Be sure to mention your hobbies and any special skills!

it's time to end a relationship when you've got the bucks and he won't sign the

Take-Me-Out Menu

What you need: Lots of bright-colored paper, a little inspiration from multi-culti take-out menus, a printer, and no shame.

What you do: Organize your best qualities by dish, then deliver to all the front doors in your neighborhood. Just sit back and wait for the phone to ring.

Sample Take-Me-Out Menu
Appetizers
Flirty Looks
Sweet Kisses
Naughty Nibbles

Main Dishes
Hot and Sizzling Me
Curry Favor Me
Vegetarian Delight Me

House Specials
Stimulating Conversation
Mouth-Watering Home-Cooked Meals
Hot Tub Hanky Panky
Warm Oil Massages
Five Years in Aromatherapy!

Dessert
Tiara ME Su
Bittersweet Chocolate Me
Handmade Mocha I Scream

Other Creative Ways to Sell Yourself . . .
* Edit a "Date Me" movie trailer on your Mac.
* Set up a kissing booth at the county fair.
* Start delicious rumors about yourself.

pre-nup. You know it's time to start a relationship when four out of your six

Keeping the Love Alive

It's date night with your steady, your hubby, or your sexy but uninspired date. What do you do to keep your love life rocking? Fanaticize and accessorize, of course! With the right props, a bad attitude, and an even badder imagination, a little role-playing will inspire a lot of playful rolling. Who puts the ass in passion and the action in attraction? You, baby!

Your roles	What you'll need	What he'll need	Keep in mind
Cabana boy and New York heiress	Sunglasses and suntan lotion	A sexy accent and a towel	No sand involved makes it much better than the real thing.
Mrs. Robinson and the Graduate	A garter belt, some black sheer stockings, and a cigarette	A nervous, eager laugh and a tie	You're in charge. And this bad young man may need a spanking as well as a few hard lessons.
Luke and Gold Bikini Leia	Gold bikini and some hairspray	A light saber and a whiny voice	If it doesn't work out, you can always bring in Hand Solo to finish the job.
Teacher and student	A red pen, a ruler, and some glasses	A bare bottom and some penitence	He wants all A's. Make him earn his top marks.

Role-play scenario	Props needed	Tip
Football player and cheerleader	Some pompons	Some shoulder pads and a jock strap	The backseat of a car is the best place to make this fantasy seem real.
Painter and subject	Your gorgeous bod and a soft spot to recline	Brushes, body paints, and patience	Steer clear of toxic paints, as licking is likely at some point.
A stripper and her john	Pasties and a pole	Dollar bills	You could actually score some cash.
Porn star and fluffer	Some lubricant and some fast hands	His own bass-heavy theme song	In the end, the fluff you make is equal to the fluff you take.
Indiana Jones and one of his blonde heroines	A blonde wig and a tight, khaki-colored outfit	A fedora hat and that famous whip	It's not the size of the whip but what you do with it!
Rock star and groupie	A concert T-shirt and some glittery lipgloss	A hard-on and no conscience	If you don't have a tour bus, a mini-van will do.
Bike messenger and executive	A tight, sexy power suit and an office with a door that locks	A messenger bag, a bulge in his biking shorts, and some sweat	He's late with your package. It's time for a special delivery payback!

Dating Tips

Dating Tip: On your second date, invite him to meet you at an indoor climbing gym. It's a great way to check out his ass from all angles—and immediately know if he's a stud or a wuss.

Dating Tip: When he asks you if you have any body art, smile seductively and confidently whisper, "All I have is body art."

Dating Tip: Want to know if he is really as confident as he seems? At a party or public social gathering, ask your date to hold your purse while you head off to the bar to freshen the drinks. If he refuses, he's a wimp. If he graciously tucks your purse under his arm and points out how well it matches his shoes and belt, he has real confidence and style.

Dating Tip: When he's super shy and has trouble talking, ask him to dance.

Dating Tip: If he keeps staring down your shirt, don't feel embarrassed and pretend not to notice. Instead, stare proudly at your gorgeous breasts, lovingly cup them and say, "Yes, are they delicious, or what?"

Dating Tip: Never throw up in your purse.

Dating Tip: When playing the field, it's best to keep several pairs of balls in the air.

Dating Tip: Confidence attracts confidence. Fun-fidence attracts everyone!

Dating Tip: Don't ever tell your mother anything negative about your boyfriend. She will never forget it.

speed dials are delivery places. You know it's time to end a relationship when

Rating Tips

Rating Tip: Be sure to rate your date at different times during the evening in various positions.

Rating Tip: Pay as much attention to the way he handles his booze as to the way he handles your boobs.

Rating Tip: In the right situation, big ears can make very nice love handles.

Rating Tip: To see how he reacts to spontaneous fun, challenge him to an impromptu game of hopscotch. Use your house keys as the markers. Winner takes all home.

Rating Tip: Want a cheat sheet of his personal style? Study his fingernails.

clear polished nails: He's a high-maintenance narcissist.

ragged nails: He's rough around the social edge.

dirty nails: He's got low self-esteem and a low account balance.

neatly trimmed short nails: He's got it together.

bitten to the quick: He's a nervous wreck.

painted black: He's a confident anarchist.

long, lady-like nails: He's . . . uh-oh!

Rating Tip: If your mother would hate him, give him 10 extra points. If your mother would date him, give him a zero.

Rating Tip: If your brother would hate him, give him 10 extra points. If your gay brother would date him, give him 20 extra points.

Rating Tip: If your best friend hates him, give him a zero. If your best friend dates him, she's a zero.

you sneeze and he says, "Do you HAVE to do that?!?" You know it's time to start

Tough Love

Getting Personal with Your Family

Is your family perfectly happy and mentally healthy? Do you feel loved, respected, adored, and understood by all your loved ones? Does the thought of your next family gathering fill you with warm fuzzies? If yes, then skip to the next section of this book or—more likely—take another dose of whatever reality-distorting drug you're on!

All families are a little nuts—and that's what makes them so much fun! Don't get down about your whacked-out, weird-ass family—get a sense of humor. Just turn your emotional dial a few notches away from seriously tragic and a few notches toward fabulously funny. Frankly, the weirder your family is, the more they have to offer you—hilarious cocktail party stories, deliciously sublime third-date answers, and thick, juicy, laugh-till-you-cry chapters in your memoirs! If you learn to laugh with and at your family, you'll be able to survive just about anything that life throws at you with confidence and style.

Note to Self: Remind family it's never too late for hush money.

a relationship when you find a guy who can make you laugh. You know it's time to

Surviving the Relation Trip

Getting along with your family is like a never-ending game of *Survivor*. Think about it. Your family is a tribe of colorful characters (some who never should be seen in a bathing suit!) all jockeying for power and immunity from blame, responsibility, and household chores. Unless you're planning to swim off to your own island (which is always an option), then you're stuck with them. The sooner you accept this and start playing the game with a winning strategy, the better you'll feel. Keep your eye on the prize—your happiness. The ultimate winner is the one who doesn't let the crazies drag her down or hold her back!

Outwit, Outplay, Outlaugh!

At your next tribal council (family dinner), suggest a few fun immunity challenges. They're a great way to bond with relatives and ease family conflicts.

Imaginative Immunity Challenges

The Challenge: Who can walk the fastest around the dining room table with the raw turkey balanced on his head? The winner earns immunity from all labor and gets to relax all day while everyone else prepares Thanksgiving dinner!

The Challenge: Who can remember your strange cousin's fiancé's name? The winner earns immunity from having to talk to either one of them all evening!

The Challenge: Who can trim the front hedge into the best topiary

end a relationship when you don't laugh together anymore. You know it's time to

animal? The winner earns immunity from ever having to trim the hedge again!

The Challenge: Who can bond with your cold, old, grumpy, rich grandpa? The winner earns immunity from being cut out of the will at the last moment!

The Challenge: Who can pack in the smallest bag for a two-week family vacation? The winner earns immunity from the family and gets to vacation at home alone!

start a relationship when your mother says, "I love it when you call, honey, but you

Stirring Up the Bad Blood!

Unless you come from a long line of bad girls, you probably scare the hell out of your family. And that can be a wonderful thing! The more your family fears you, the more freedom you'll have to be as bad as you want to be. Live all of your life without all of their strife. Here are a few proven techniques for getting your family to run from you and write you off as unreformable.

How to Freak Out Your Family

* Shave your head.
* Videotape all family discussions for your upcoming docu-drama.
* Join a cult.
* Ask deep, probing, personal questions and calmly wait for an answer.
* Fall madly in love with the "wrong kind of" person. (Gleefully show up at all family gatherings with him/her.)
* Start quoting the Bible.
* Join the Junior League.
* Punctuate your debate point by flashing your nipple piercings.
* When they disapprove of what you wear/say/do for a living, say, "Thank you!"
* Change religions.
* Don't just mow the lawn, Mohawk the lawn.
* Ask if they want their names changed in your coming-of-rage memoir.
* Tell them you've had your tubes tied.

called this morning." You know it's time to end a relationship when your mother

Wild Ways to Get through Wacko Family Gatherings

* Manic hobbies (beading, knitting, jigsaw puzzles, frantic potato mashing, Xbox, macaroni mosaics)

* Drink heavily.

* Lots of long out-of-body experiences

* Drugs

* Volunteer to sit at the kids' table.

* Hole up in front of a computer, doing online "research" for your big, imaginary presentation at work.

* Run out of gas on the way and never arrive!

* Hide in a closet for a few hours.

starts every sentence with "I don't want to meddle, but have you noticed . . ."

Find the Bad Girls!

DysFUNctional Family Therapy

Who needs to pay for family therapy when you can play for family therapy? When you initiate the right recreational activities, blood pressure, tempers, and voices will rise while dysfunctional dynasties fall. In no time, you'll be clearing the air or calling 911. Either way, something's going to blow!

Fun Things to Do with Your Dysfunctional Family

Just because your family is a little psycho doesn't mean you can't still have tons of fun together.

* Drive around getting lost.
* Double date.
* Frantically shop on Christmas Eve.
* Spend a family vacation in rehab.
* Sell tickets to ride the big pink elephant in the room.
* Spill your guts on a national talk show.
* Imitate each other's tics, quirks, and most annoying qualities.
* Rent movies about families more screwed up than yours! (It's a great way to inspire casual family chats on deep, painful topics—or at least feel a whole lot better about your messed-up family.)
* Go to church every Sunday and pretend to be perfect.
* Play hide-the-credit-card. (It's a gas watching those shopaholics gets the jitters!)
* Practice your new hobby—knife throwing!

Wonderfully Whacked Family Movies

All about My Mother

American Beauty

Blood Simple

Bottle Rocket

But I'm a Cheerleader

Cat on a Hot Tin Roof

Dead Ringers

Desert Hearts

Down and Out in Beverly Hills

East of Eden

The First Wives Club

The Godfather

Happiness

Home for the Holidays

Indochine

The Lover

Magnolia

Mommie Dearest

Ordinary People

Parenthood

The Royal Tenenbaums

Ruthless People

A Simple Plan

Throw Mama from the Train

Who's Afraid of Virginia Woolf?

Pruning Your Family Tree

There's funny crazy in families and then there's unfunny, unhealthy crazy. Be smart enough to know the difference and strong enough to snip it in the bad bud. You can't choose your family—but you can choose not to play their twisted, little games. Don't play along with nasty-ass family members or family games that leave you feeling used and abused or just plain polluted with toxic goo. Break free, get away, get perspective, get help, and get on with your bad girl life.

Un-fun Games Families Play
Just say NO to these crazy family games!

Hide and Shriek: Why talk about those icky, messy feelings when you can keep them neatly hidden until you explode like a nuclear family bomb?

Tattleship: Direct communication is such a drag! We'd much rather narc on you, gossip behind your back, and fire vicious verbal bombs!

We're Not Sorry!: Why should we apologize for royally screwing you up as a child? Thanks to our healthy program of fun pharmaceuticals and relaxing fermented beverages, we can't remember a thing! Cheers, here's to us!

Guide that you don't already own. You know it's time to end a relationship when

MANopoly: When the guys have all the power, it's a tired, old bored game—just like us! Do not pass go, do not be taken seriously, do not control your own money, do not own property, do not have opinions that matter—unless you have a penis!

Capture the Fag: All social and sexual deviants will be held prisoner and emotionally tortured until broken . . . er, rather . . . cured! "What are we supposed to tell our friends about you!?"

Not a Clue: I know nothing, I see nothing, I hear nothing. I don't want to know what Colonel Mustard is doing with the candlestick in the kitchen! I'd much rather keep my pretty little head in the sand where it's quiet and safe.

Squabble: Use your words (big words, small words, curse words) to score points against your loved ones. Wahoo! It's family fun for everyone when you scream and yell all the time about nothing!

Your Trivial Pursuits: Since we love you soooo much, we're going to save you from a miserable life of suffering and failure by telling you over and over that you're an idiot. Honey, you're wasting your time on that ridiculous person/job/plan. You'll never accomplish that stupid goal. Yippee! Isn't this game fun!

Note to Self: Family getaway? No. Family, get away? Yes!

you've been dating for years and you're afraid to fart within a hundred yards of

How to Bond with Your Bad Girl Granny

Just because she's getting a little old and shriveled doesn't mean her bad girl desires have shriveled up, too! Your grandmother will be thrilled and delighted when you reach out and treat her like a bad girl friend. Be sure to take notes. You'll not only be laughing a lot, you'll be learning a lot.

* Sneak her cigarettes and bourbon.
* Ask her to tell you her secret bad girl desires.
* Join her knitting circle and teach her friends to knit skimpy bikinis.
* Take her shopping for vibrators ("Modern technology, oh my!").
* Help her set up her computer and keep it running smoothly.
* Ask her to tell that "I was a lesbian once, during the war" story again.
* Take her and a few bad friends to a racy movie, or badder yet, to Chippendales.
* Road trip with her to Vegas!
* Give each other home perms.
* Play strip-bridge.
* At her next birthday party, teach everyone the bad girl dance.
* Swap dirty jokes.
* Swap pick-up stories, tips, and techniques.
* Take her to the track and gamble the day away.
* Keep her laughing.

him. You know it's time to start a relationship when you look forward to your

Things to Do with . . . Self-Help Books

* Use as emergency toilet paper on the road

* Throw an Accept Yourself Party and invite all your equally dysfunctional pals over for mojitos and a self-help bonfire

* Press wildflowers

* Paper-train your adorable new puppy

* Drill holes through hard covers, load onto a broomstick, soak in cold water, and then do arm curls and bench presses

* Cut into confetti for your next pity party

* Plant a stack in your evil boss's or co-worker's office before that important client's next visit

* Cut into strips and make bad girl pom pons

* Use an X-Acto knife to cut out the center of all the pages. Transform it into a festive candy dish or convenient stash box to hide your baddie items in plain view.

* Keep on your nightstand to throw at unwanted intruders

* Carry a really pathetic title in your bag so you can whip out and scare off any skeevy guy

* Use for kindling on romantic weekend getaways

* Read aloud at parties as a drinking game (Whenever a book tells you to do something stupid, everyone takes a sip.)

* Wrap nicely and give (back) to evil relatives

* Mail to the White House

annual gyno exam because it's the only action you've seen all year. You know it's

Managing Your Parents

Parents are like old shoes: the sooner you start conditioning them to like you, the longer they'll be around to comfortably support you. Your parents really don't need any more of your grief or criticism, what they really need is your compassion. When you reach out and make an effort to improve your relationship, you can help them and help yourself!

But keep in mind, parents are like children; they not only need boundaries, they want them.

It's Not Easy Being a Parent . . .

They are suffering from Empty Nest Egg Syndrome.

Their butts are sagging.

They can't read a menu even with their glasses.

Tattoos scare them.

The music they love is totally uncool.

They can't open a PDF file.

They think freelance is the same thing as being unemployed.

Their memory is going and they often forget your name.

They can't figure out the digital cable remote.

They think Pilates is a band.

And they still don't know the answers to life's biggest questions!

Note to Self: Don't forget to have a baby so someone will make jokes at your expense when you're old and feeble.

time to end a relationship when you start referring to him as "the dead fish."

The Parent Translator

Don't let a little generation gap become a communication barrier. With a slight adjustment to your parental hearing aid, you can understand everything your parents say!

What they say:

Are you saving enough?

You could get arrested in that outfit.

Are you being safe?

Your sister would never say that to us.

When I was your age, I was married with three children.

If you're exploring that gay stuff, do not tell a soul.

With that attitude, you're going to be out of the will.

We've fallen in love all over again.

When are you getting married?

Are you taking good care of yourself and eating right?

What they mean:

Are you saving enough to support me when I'm old?

Damn, I wish I still had a body like yours.

Don't expect me to raise that baby while your single-mother ass goes to work every day!

Your sister's a bore.

I wish I had had that much fun. Do-over!

If you're exploring that gay stuff, do not tell me!

We got hammered in the stock market crash.

We are so happy that you finally moved out!

When can we throw a big party for all our friends?

Will I be getting a grandchild soon?

Other Reasons to Be Really Nice to Your Parents:

the country club
the beach house
the ski cabin
the will
the liquor cabinet
electronic hand-me-downs
the boat
season tickets
free baby-sitting
random care packages
mom's pot roast

Badder Bonding with Mom

Whether you never get along with your mother or always get along with her, your relationship is guaranteed to be complicated. Don't just accept that—celebrate it! Since you can't stay completely away from the twists and turns in a mother-daughter relationship, learn to maneuver them like a confident pro, avoiding those gnarly emotional wipeouts and breakdowns.

Worst Thing to Say to Get Back at Your Mother

"You're just like Grandma."

You know it's time to start a relationship when you get into fights with your

Wicked Ways to Get BAD with Your Mother:

* Hit the road! Drive to nearest truck stop and drink bad coffee, eat good pie, and share your secret bad girl desires.
* Take her to the firing range and shoot guns.
* Get matching tattoos. It's the perfect payback for all those matching outfits she made you wear.
* Drive to grandma and grandpa's and T.P. their house.
* Drag her to the local cosmetics counter for a baddy makeover, then on to a hip salon where you get to art direct her new look. (Don't forget the duct tape to keep her quiet.)
* Take her on a drive down memory lane and get her to reenact her baddest exploits from her teenage years. (If she doesn't have any, then take a drive down your memory lane.)
* Open a bottle of good wine, pop in the home videos from old family vacations, and narrate them until you can't stop laughing and/or crying.
* Host a mother-and-daughter tea for two, and swap clothes, hairstyles, attitudes, personas, and stories all afternoon.
* Get out the paints and do loving, hilarious portraits of each other.
* Plant some pot—of course, for medicinal purposes only—in between the petunias and see if dad ever notices.
* Spend all day in the kitchen cooking and/or baking your most sinfully indulgent recipes.
* Plan a Baddy Awards night for her friends and yours. And do it!

imaginary boyfriend. You know it's time to end a relationship when your pet

Are You My Mother?
No really, are you? 'Cause you're scaring me!

Does your mother constantly annoy you, embarrass you, or just plain freak you out? Do you suddenly wonder if aliens have invaded her body and her brain? Do you find yourself secretly wishing that you were adopted? If so, then you could be suffering from Mid-Life-Mama Drama. The bad news—your mother's midlife crisis could last 20 to 30 years. The good news—it's a tragic but rarely terminal condition that affects mothers of all ages. A quick review will show you how to deal.

Groovy Mom
Her jeans are too tight, her shorts are too short, and her sexy halter top fits her juuuuu-ust right! She loves to dance and sing to Britney Spears (yuck!). She tries so hard to be cool, fashionable, and with-it that you end up feeling like some stuffy loser.

Bossy Mom
She has an unsolicited opinion on everything! She tells you and everyone else exactly what to do in order to be happy and fulfilled because she sure as hell isn't.

Buddy Mom
She desperately wants to be your breast

bites him and you're not sorry. You know it's time to start a relationship when you

friend—and tells you inappropriate details about her finances, sex life, relationships, secret crushes, and even recurring sex dreams. (Eeew!)

Martyr Mom
The only joy she gets from life is suffering—and telling everyone about it in vivid detail.

Slutty Mom
Who puts the "ho" in homemaker? Your mom! That's who.

Nosey Mom
Gossip is her only currency. Unless she knows everything about everyone's personal business, she feels empty, bereft, and worthless. (And frankly, she is.)

Nazi Mom
On a good day, she's the fun police. The rest of the time, she's a controlling, overbearing, miserable meanie who loves to lay down the law because it's the only way she gets laid anymore.

No matter what type of mother you have, she's the only one you have. So get personal with her. If she's part of a bad cycle, help her break it and get her groove on. If she's part of a bad girl cycle, help her celebrate it.

seriously think about getting a third cat. You know it's time to end a relationship

You're Never Too Old to Blame Your Mother

Your Problem

You're a sex addict.

Big credit card debt

Facial hair

Your tarantula tattoo is crawling out of a bridesmaid dress.

You don't trust men.

Food

Your religion is shopping.

Your Explanation

"Mom didn't breast feed me long enough!"

"It's not my fault. The first two words I learned to say were 'Charge it!'"

"My mother's Italian."

"I never even wanted a tattoo until mom forbid me to get one!"

"If mom hadn't married such an asshole . . . "

"My mother always kept the pantry locked. How sick is that?"

"My mother believed in a higher credit limit and worshipped at its altar every day."

You know the words to every Barry Manilow song.

Sexual inhibition and shame

You have to color your hair every month.

You're a bossy backseat driver.

You scare people.

"I had a tragic childhood. My mother would dance around the house vacuuming and singing to Barry Manilow."

"How would you feel if your mom always said, 'Don't touch your pee pee! Don't touch your pee pee!'?"

"My mother still insists I'm a blonde to prove that she's a blonde."

"Mom made me ride in the backseat until I was sixteen."

"My mother was a bad girl."

Building a Badder Relationship with Dad

Before you can improve your relationship with your father, you have to take a stab at understanding him. This requires an honest and often painful assessment of his capabilities and relationship skills.

Emotional IQ Pop Quiz

How does your dad measure up?

Score each category with a number from 1 to 10. (Ten is the best.)

__ **Emotional Intelligence:** He really understands his feelings and yours.

__ **Emotional Diligence:** He works hard to express his feelings and hear yours.

__ **Emotional Ignorance:** He has no clue what you're even talking about.

__ **Emotional Flatulence:** When discussing feelings, he's full of hot air, and his comments really stink.

__ **Emotional Abstinence:** He's taken a vow never to feel anything ever again.

__ **Emotional Excellence:** He's in touch with his feelings, respects yours, and can talk about it without cocktails.

This little Pop Quiz was really just to distract you and give you the illusion of parental influence. Bottom line—Your father is doing the best he can! You can't teach him, coach him, change him . . . unless he really wants to change himself. And like that's really going to happen! Who wants to think about emotions when you can be watching football?

when you start checking out online dating websites "just for curiosity." You

The Daddy Decoder

If your father is old school, he probably doesn't like to talk about his feelings; he prefers to yell about them. But once you accept this about him, you can take a few steps back, slip on your emotional flak jacket, and stop taking it personally. If your father is new age, he probably can't stop talking about his feelings, which sometimes is more annoying than saying nothing at all.

Old-School Dad

When he feels . . .	He shows . . .
hurt	anger
sad	anger
insecure	anger
love	his wallet
frustrated	anger
fearful	anger
happy	his wallet
jealous	anger
broke	anger
embarrassed	anger
confident	his wallet
rejected	anger
confused	anger
challenged	anger
proud	his wallet
old	anger
misunderstood	anger
tired	anger

know it's time to start a relationship when your only three-way fantasy is with

New-Age Dad

There is nothing more annoying than a father whose new favorite hobby is getting in touch with his emotions. Usually this follows a near-death experience or a stock market crash. The good news—it's just a phase he's going through and it will probably pass.

How to Spot a New Age Dad

He starts wearing Birkenstocks to work.

He has given up coffee and the *Wall Street Journal* and now meditates each morning.

He wants to talks about everything.

He's wearing jewelry and carrying a man bag.

He says strange things like, "Right on." "I acknowledge your pain." "I can hear where you're coming from." "Please pass the Enya CD."

He doesn't just want to hear about your date, he wants to go with you—even if you're thirty-five!

He eats tofu by choice.

He invites you to a father-daughter yoga retreat.

If your father is showing any of these symptoms, he could be a dangerous influence on you. It's best to keep your distance until the phase passes and he goes back to drinking and golf.

How to Talk with Your Father

If your father is like most men, he has been conditioned for decades to fear and loathe talking to a woman. Even though you are his sweet, innocent, darling daughter, subliminally he cannot separate you from all of the women who have used words to hurt him, humiliate him, and trap him.

Fortunately, bonding with your father may not have anything to do with verbal communication as you know it. In fact, if he's old school, the less you talk to your dad, the better! Try joining in on a few of these Daddy Dearest activities. When your dad is doing something he enjoys, he may not even notice that you're having a conversation. Who knows, over time he might actually become conditioned and associate your heart-to-heart chats with pleasure, relaxation, and fun.

Ways to Bond with Dear, Old Dad

* Drink.
* Smoke cigars.
* Work on the car.
* Play golf.
* Play poker.
* Watch sports.
* Go bowling.
* Gamble.
* Pull weeds.
* Discuss the stock market.
* Shoot baskets.
* Admire his train layout.

a third person in the relationship to spice things up. You know it's time to start a

Sibling Chivalry

Sibling rivalry is so common. It requires no imagination, no finesse, no creativity. In the garden of families, it's the low-hanging fruit. Sibling chivalry is the new cool. Think about it. Whether you're staying out late, spending your retirement money on shoes, or going to Hawaii (not sick at home) instead of going to the crazy cousin's reunion, who is most likely to narc on you? Your sibling, that's who! The sooner you get your brothers and sisters on your side, the better and badder your life will be.

Reasons to Get Personal and Friendly with Your Siblings:

* Finally, someone sides with you
* It will freak out your parents.
* Better gifts on birthdays and holidays
* Someone to share the cost of your parents' long-term care
* Potential blood or organ donor

Sibling chivalry is most satisfy-ing when you and your brother or sister are totally different. Don't resent your siblings for being different from you—respect and celebrate them! As much as they may bug the hell out of you, who they are creates an oppor-tunity for you to be you.

relationship when he buys you the toothbrush to keep at his house. You know it's

If your sibling is the popular one, then you get to be the mysterious child.

If your sibling is impossibly pretty, then you get to be the impossibly brainy child.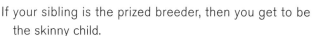

If your sibling is the loser under-achiever, then you get to be the uncontested "most-favored child"!

If your sibling is the prized breeder, then you get to be the skinny child.

If your sibling is the annoyingly successful overachiever, then you get a responsible co-signer on your first mortgage and someone to bail you out of jail!

Friendships in your life will come and go, but friendships with your siblings are for life. Building a badder relationship is as easy as one, two, three:

Make amends. Apologize for putting his head in the toilet and making him eat cat food. Youthful indiscretion!

Make friends. Find some common interests/people/vices and then enjoy them together.

Make a pact. Agree to pretend that you have no idea what your parents are talking about.

And don't forget, your siblings might produce children that you can win over to the Bad Side . . . .

How to Be the Cool Aunt

A loving, dedicated bad girl knows it's her duty and honor to be the cool aunt and shed some bad girl light on nieces and nephews, whether at a family outing or a

time to end a relationship when after a year you still don't feel comfortable letting

baby-sitting gig. What makes a bad girl aunt so cool? She tells it like it is. She's got the guts to talk about things that scare off most people. She gives the straight scoop and the real poop—no matter how embarrassing. She colors outside the lines. She introduces her BGITs (bad girls in training) to different types of people, different ideas, different experiences, and different shoe stores!

Bad Things to Do with Your BGIT Niece

* Dance around the house in your underwear. (Be sure to teach her the Bad Girl Dance!)
* Have a Pig-Out Party and worship your bulging Buddha bellies.
* Smuggle homemade popcorn into a movie theater.
* Style your hair super big, drive to a truck stop, and eat pancakes for dinner.
* Do hilarious impressions of parents, teachers, bosses, and other authority figures.
* Play poker for jelly beans, tampons, or colored condoms.
* Have a slumber party, stay up really late, and talk about boys, boobs, and other personal stuff.
* Learn to yodel.
* Build a personal power shrine.
* Go to a political protest.
* Transform pantyliners and tampons into groovy, glittery earrings, bracelets, and necklaces.
* Go shoe shopping!
* Take turns flattening your scale with a sledgehammer.

him see you without makeup. You know it's time to start a relationship because

* Use Jell-O to dye your hair pink, purple, orange, or green. (Tons o' fun before family gatherings!)

Bad Things to Teach Your BFF Niece

* It's not your bottom, it's your sweet lovin' booty caboose!
* You don't need a passport to French kiss.
* If you listen very quietly, you can hear the sound of the ocean in your shoes.
* It's better to be hippy and happy than skinny and meany.
* An appetite for everything is a good thing.
* Underwear is overrated.
* Blue eye shadow is never a good idea.
* A boob job will never pay well enough to support you.
* A hand job does not pay at all.
* It's much badder to be the exception than the rule.
* Cocktail hour actually lasts two hours (three hours for WASPs).
* Masturbating does not make you go blind (but it can cause carpal tunnel syndrome).
* A scar is actually your very own, very personal, very sexy body art.
* Cheese is tasty mold.
* Real women have real bodies—not perfect bodies.
* It's much easier to tell the truth than it is to live a lie.
* Buy the expensive tweezers. They're worth it.
* You do not have to be skinny to skinny dip.

Note to self: Parents are not always right—but they need to think they are.

you just know. You know it's time to end a relationship when you keep wondering

Casual Love

Getting Personal with Your Crew

A bad girl is never stingy with her love. (That would be so cruel!) She doesn't hoard it, hide it, or save it for later. She knows that all you need is love, and love is the answer to every big social-life question. A bad girl always has an open mind, an open heart, and an open container of casual love ready to serve up to anyone she meets.

Casual love is like casual sex—without the mess or the messy consequences. It's a flirt, a smile, a smirk, a deep penetrating glance, an unexpected dance. It's taking a small risk to reach out and make someone think, laugh, or feel some heat. Casual love is giving someone extra special attention with no strings attached.

Casual love is . . .	Casual love is not . . .
playful and fun.	painful for anyone.
flashing a special smile.	flashing your drunk tits.
making anyone feel special.	making anyone feel cheap.
slipping in some personal style.	slipping in some tongue.
spreading your Baddy Sauce.	spreading your legs.
getting everyone thinking.	getting everyone drinking.
blowing him a kiss.	blowing him.
leaving a wake of wild experiences.	lying awake in a wet experience.

what you would do if you accidentally fell in love with someone else. You know

Spreading the casual love is simple, really. It's just taking a personal interest in someone you barely know. It's showing a little affection to a perfect stranger. It's serving up a little tenderness and going the extra mile to make a real connection. It's the ultimate form of unconditional love. No guilt. No embarrassment. No fear. No expectations. No promises. No worries. No STDs.

Why show the world your casual love? Why not? It's good, clean fun and it's free! With a little guts and bad girl attitude, you can turbo-charge your most casual relationships. What are you waiting for?

Note to Self: Life is short—love hard!

Anonymous Quickies

Why settle for "Have a nice day" when you can make someone's day? All you need is a little You Goo, a little humor, and a lot of style to shower everyone you meet with casual love. Here are a few tips for how to transform any brief chance encounter into a perfect relationship.

Mammogram Technician

When you open your blouse, your heart, and your humor, you can be breast friends in minutes!

Be Positive: Smile lovingly and whisper, "My boyfriend has been away, so don't mind me if enjoy this a little. Okay?"

Be Supportive: "Do you enjoy working with your hands? Of course, you do! You are gooooood!"

Be Provocative: "Bet I can guess your favorite vegetable . . . Boob squash!"

it's time to start a relationship when you find someone who brings out the

Toll Booth Operator

He's not a machine; he's a person with a heart and feelings just like you. Don't just pass the buck, pass the love!

Be Positive: Smile and enthusiastically yell, "Hello, beautiful person!"

Be Supportive: "Nice hands! Do you moisturize?"

Be Provocative: Flash a sign that reads, "Make Change Not War!" and give him the thumbs up. Pass your toll and a sweet love letter.

Traffic Cop

Behind that gun and those reflective sunglasses is a gentle soul looking for a little love and acceptance.

Be Positive: "Wow. That uniform makes you look buff and very handsome." (Works great for male or female cops!)

Be Supportive: "I'm so glad you pulled me over. We really should get together more often."

Be Provocative: When he (or she) walks away from your car, whistle and say in a deep, throaty voice, "What do I have to do to get you to handcuff me?"

Cab Driver

Just because you're separated by a Plexiglas barrier doesn't mean you can't connect.

Be Positive: Make eye contact in the mirror, smile warmly, and say, "Gee, your hair smells terrific!"

Be Supportive: "Whatever route you take, I am behind you all the way!"

best version of you. You know it's time to end a relationship when his idea of

Be Provocative: Draw a heart with lipstick on the Plexiglas barrier. "Your pheromones are driving me crazy!"

Sales Girl

She's on her feet all day. So why make her do all the work when you can meet her halfway?

Be Positive: "Oh, my God! Those pants make your butt look super cute!"

Be Supportive: "That color is so you! You must be a summer."

Be Provocative: "Psssst! Trade you a foot massage for your employee discount."

DMV Employee

With a little baditude adjustment, you can transform the DMV into a TLC pleasure palace.

Be Positive: To stand out in the crowd and show you care, always bring a gift. (DMV favorites: Twinkies, donuts, Happy Meals)

Be Supportive: Wear a push-up bra and sexy low-cut top and be sure to lean on the counter. Everyone enjoys a beautiful view, especially when trapped under fluorescent lights all day long.

Be Provocative: "Pssst! I have a confession: I memorized the eye chart and I don't even wear glasses!"

listening is nodding and looking over your shoulder. You know it's time to start

Repair Man

You've always secretly wondered what makes a handy-man so handy. Keep wondering. Remember: If it isn't broken, don't fix it.

Be Positive: "Wow! Your butt crack looks really clean!"

Be Supportive: "Can I fix you a strong cup of coffee so you'll move a little faster?"

Be Provocative: "I can't help myself. I just love a man in a Maytag uniform."

Bank Teller

With a little fun-ancial planning, you can add excitement and fun to any bank teller's day.

Be Positive: When you step up to the window, act nervous, look both ways, and slip her a note that reads, "You're my favorite teller in the whole wide world!"

Be Supportive: "You've got the power to make that little overdraft charge go away. And I really respect and support women with power."

Be Provocative: Before going to the bank, write "Open for Badness" on a pantyliner. When your banking business is complete, casually slap the pantyliner up next to the teller's window. She'll be getting big smiles from customers for the rest of the day!

Cable Guy

Hey, he's the man with the van and he's been authorized to check your box. What more do you need to know to build a special relationship?

Be Positive: "Hello there. I've been waiting all day for a man like you."

a relationship when there is only one (growing) butt indentation on your sofa.

Be Supportive: "My last cable guy only had the basic package, but I can see you've got the premium package."
Be Provocative: "I love the tattoo on your right cheek!"

Airport Security Guard

The next time you're pulled out of line for special treatment, why act annoyed and put upon when you can act hot and turned on? Airport security has never felt so bad!
Be Positive: Before going through the metal detector, take off more than your coat, belt, and shoes—take it all off! When you strip down to your teeny bikini, you show everyone that you take airport security seriously.
Be Supportive: Wink, smile, and whisper, "Thanks, I needed that. I've been feeling really stressed lately."
Be Provocative: During the pat down, moan like you mean it, then shout in ecstasy, "Yeah, yeah, right there. Don't move. Faster, faster, yes, yes, YES!"

Cubicle-Enslaved Payment Processor

When you include a juicy personal note with your payment, you can show your personality and show another human being that you truly care.
Be Positive: "I wanted to pay on time but I just got out of a coma!"

You know it's time to end a relationship when you have a sexual dream about

Be Supportive: "I would totally understand if you added a zero or two to my payment amount. In fact, I would be your new best friend!" (Be sure to draw two smiley faces holding hands.)

Be Provocative: "You don't have to charge me that late fee, do you? Instead why don't you picture me writing this check to you in the nude! Ooh, yeah. Doesn't that feel much, much better?"

Customer Service Rep

Inject a little You Goo through the phone lines and transform an anonymous nobody into a somebody special!

Be Positive: "I hope I'm not being too forward, Brian/Pat/Laqueesha, but your breath smells really fresh!"

Be Supportive: "Can I speak to your manager? I want to recommend you for employee of the year."

Be Provocative: In a seductive whisper, ask, "Can you guess what I'm wearing now? My telephone headset!"

People in Line

Why have a cold, out-of-body experience when you can have a hot, everybody experience? The next time you're waiting in line with some sexy strangers, go ahead and cross the line!

Be Positive: "Excuse me. You're butt looks really good in those pants. How's mine look?"

Be Supportive: "At least we're not at the unemployment office! Wait, are we?"

Be Provocative: "If we lived in line, we'd be living together by now!"

Wait

Every bad girl wants to be on time, all the time. But your life is full, your schedule is jam packed, and who understands time anyway? Late happens! When you're the tardy party, you feel guilty, stressed, and pressed for a good excuse. When you're the baddie in waiting, you feel dissed—disrespected, disappointed, and disenchanted. Either way it stinks.

What's a late girl to do? You've tried to plan your deals ahead, but no matter what you do, you just can't lose the wait. That's where Bad Girl Wait Watchers comes in—it's a revolutionary wait-loss system that helps you take the wait off and keep it off, because as the Duchess of Bad says, "Nothing tastes as good as being on time feels."

In Wait Watchers, every punctuality-related activity is assigned a point value—based on a combination of minutes you make them wait, location, and type of event. You'll be given a daily point target based on your wait history, a journal to track your daily progress, and a POINTSfinder that spells out how many points each activity is worth. Remember to factor in activity points for your proactive attempts at being on time and 35 extra flex points per week that you can use for those inevitable time challenges that we all face.

One day a week you and the bad girls in your local Wait Watchers group must get together and weigh in on your progress. Inspirational wait-loss stories and timeliness tips are always welcome.

kissing and get mad. You know it's time to end a relationship when you start

Watchers

Note to Self: Write book on time mismanagement?

collecting his hair and toenail clippings to make that voodoo doll. You know it's

Wait Watchers POINTS finder

making friend wait . . .

10 minutes	1 point
for every additional 5 minutes, add	1 point
if at food court in mall, add	2 points
if on cold, windy corner, add	3 points
if at already rushed lunch hour, add	3 points
if she had to drive to you, add	3 points
if she had to pay to park, add	4 points
if at a skeevy bar, add	5 points
if at a skeevy bar filled with sexy, hot, dangerous-looking guys, add	0 points
if you were late last time, add	5 points
if she was late last time, add	1 point
if late on her birthday, add	6 points

being late for . . .

church	1 point
yoga class	1 point
your period	3 points
work	2 points
important meeting	3 points
hot date	4 points
study date	1 point
doctor's appointment	1 point
hair appointment	2 points
facial	2 points
birthday parties	5 points
graduations	4 points
movie	3 points
plane flight	5 points
kick-boxing class	2 points

zero-point activities *(so awful you're rewarded just for showing up)*

evil step-parent's birthday party	0 points

bar/bat mitzvahs	0 points
DMV appointments	0 points
paying your taxes on time	0 points
gynecologist appointment	0 points
writing college essays	0 points
blind date	0 points
dentist appointment	0 points
paying parking ticket before increased fine	0 points
airport pick-up service	0 points
waiting for cable or phone repair	0 points
office party or picnic	0 points
meeting to exchange belongings with your ex	0 points
baby shower	0 points
birthday party for friend's pet/toddler	0 points
your boyfriend's high school reunion	0 points
shopping for a friend's wedding dress	0 points
bikini wax	0 points
bathing suit shopping	0 points
family Thanksgiving dinner	0 points
shipping packages at the post office during the holidays	0 points
time spent adding up points	0 points

activity points *(subtract a point for these positive moves)*

coming up with a really good excuse	-1 point
being honest	-1 point
getting there early and securing a booth	-1 point
being on time for reservations	-1 point
making reservations	-1 point
not hitting the snooze bar	-1 point
not parking in a handicap spot just to make it	-1 point
not getting a parking ticket	-1 point
not getting a speeding ticket	-1 point
talking your way out of a speeding ticket	-3 points
remembering birthdays and other holidays	-1 point
going to the gym	-1 point

Your Personal Pit Crew

Even a bad girl can't do it alone. Whether you are cruising in the fast lane or parked in the pink zone, you need the loving support of skilled professionals to keep your bad girl lifestyle running smoothly. With just a bit of Bad Girl attention and a little squeeze of You Goo, every support person in your pit crew will feel like the star of your show.

Getting Personal with Your Therapist

The truth is, your therapist doesn't want to hear another thing about your problems, fears, phobias, or all the mean-ass people who have done you wrong. Of course, she'll never say that because she wants to be polite and she needs your business. Despite the advanced degrees and serious demeanor, your therapist actually wants to enjoy the next fifty minutes of her life—just like you. And frankly, she gets tired of having to do all the work in your relationship. If you would analyze her and ask the deep, probing questions every once in a while, you'd offer her a refreshing change of pace. More than anything, your therapist would love a good laugh, a good story, and a good touch of the crazies!

Before the session . . .

* Using a soft eye pencil, write "LUV" on your right eyelid and "YOU" on the left lid. If she asks you about it, tell her she's projecting again.
* Tape record a loop of provocative messages on a microcassette recorder, then hide it and leave it on "play" for the duration of your therapy session.

time to start a relationship when you've created a chart of your friends' love lives

Possible messages to record:

"I'm sorry, but our time is up."

"Red rum. Red rum. Red rum."

"I know you understand it, but how does it make you feel?"

"I don't actually have health insurance. Ha ha ha!"

"Does that remind you of your mother?"

When she asks you about the recorded messages, act surprised and concerned, then sincerely ask how long she's been hearing voices.

During the session . . .

* Every now and then, speak in pig Latin.
* Stretch out on the sofa and take a nap.
* Repeat everything she says, imitating her voice and cadence.
* Randomly change your friends', lovers', and parents' names to keep her on her toes.
* Excuse yourself to go to the bathroom. Don't come back.

Getting Personal with Your Gynecologist

The typical gynecologist spends most days with her head in someone's crotch. Of course, as a professional she's all business and acts as if it's a totally normal thing to do. But deep down inside she's kind of embarrassed. (Come on, wouldn't you be?) During a pelvic exam, your gynecologist secretly wants to laugh out loud or at least be distracted and amused while she works. With a little planning and a lot of imagination, you can entertain and thrill your gynecologist. You'll be her favorite patient in no time! Remember, if you're relaxed and having fun, your

and call to get all the kinky details. You know it's time to end a relationship when

gyno will be, too. Here are just a few fun-filled suggestions to make your next pap smear a happy schmear.

Before the exam . . .

* Tease your bush into a pageboy, pompadour, or Bozo the Clown do. Then spray for maximum hold.
* If you're sporting a Brazilian, draw big ears and a smiley face with a felt-tip pen.
* Adhere a few sticky notes to your inner thighs with to-do lists like "buy milk, get lube job and oil change, find lost boyfriend."
* Throw her a few curve balls, and leave last night's ben-wa balls in place.
* Spritz your privates with perfume or eau de toilette.

During the exam . . .

* Each time she tells you to scoot down a little farther, make a little farting sound.
* Ask her how she chose this line of work.
* Impress her with your memorized rendition of the Gettysburg Address.
* Shoot rubber bands off the ceiling. Three points if you can get one through the stirrups without hitting your gyno.
* Play Twenty Questions.
* Suck on a helium balloon and read haiku poetry.
* Ask her to keep an eye out for that thong you can't seem to find.

Getting Personal with Your IRS Agent

A tax audit is the perfect opportunity to build a special bond with your IRS agent and share an unforgettable intimate experience. Most people don't realize that an IRS agent wants to be loved—not feared—by everyone around him. He or she may look like an uptight, humorless bean counter, but underneath it all is a fun-loving sexual being, longing to be enticed from his cage. He'll never admit it, but your IRS agent has an animal appetite and a naughty sense of humor.

Before the audit . . .

* Turn up the heat in the room where you'll be reviewing your tax return. (A few delicate beads of sweat will set the mood!)
* Be sure to wear a low-cut top.
* Insert a few provocative photos of you and a friend into the stack of receipts.
* Have a shot of whiskey. (If the IRS agent can smell liquor on your breath, he'll think of his favorite bar and have a positive association to you.)

During the audit . . .

* When you can't find receipts for all your deductions, use the term "barter system" as often as possible. Most IRS agents really respect ingenuity and creative financing.
* Sit very close to your IRS agent. Accidentally let your thigh brush against his thigh. When he or she inches away, you casually follow. Don't be afraid to scoot all the way around the table. IRS agents love little games like this!
* Compliment him on his tie and the color of his eyes.

he calls you "Mommy." You know it's time to start a relationship when becoming

* When he or she asks, "Do you think this is a joke?," smile and ask, "Are you flirting with me? You devil."
* Sneeze frequently into his coffee or water glass. Then whisper, "So sorry. My allergies kick up when I'm near a powerful man."
* Touch his shoulder for emphasis, then say, "Do you work out?"
* When he asks a question that you can't or don't want to answer, lean toward him, look down pretending to think hard, and check out your beautiful breasts. Then look up quickly, catching him in the same act, and innocently say, "I'm sorry, I'm confused. Are you asking about my business assets or my personal assets?"
* Ask him to show you how fast he is on his calculator.

If You Have to Break Up with . . .

Your Therapist: Leave a drunken hysterical voicemail message late at night: "It's over! It's over! Admit it, you're seeing other people."

Your Bartender: Throw a drink in his face and walk out.

Your Mechanic: Leave a tool kit on his hood with a work order telling him to screw himself.

Your Barista: "Beans! Beans! I can't take this grind any more."

Your Gynecologist: "Cold speculum, cold heart."

Your IRS Agent: Send a Dear John letter via Certified Mail.

Your Meter Maid: Leave a note under her windshield wiper—and a Denver boot on her scooter tire.

---

a nun sounds like a super career move for your lifestyle. You know it's time to

* Act shocked and embarrassed when you discover those provocative photos again and again and again.

Getting Personal with Your Meter Maid

Everyone hates the local meter maid, except ingenious you! The next time you see your meter maid, don't scowl, growl, or flash the one-finger salute—instead smile and wave like a friendly goober. Then introduce yourself as if you have just moved into the area. Get her name and make sure she gets yours. Then ask about her family and what she likes to do outside of work. And, naturally, ask for her best (legal) parking tips. Be sure you see her while driving your car so you can honk and wave madly so she'll know the make and model you drive. Once you build a friendly relationship, then it's time to get personal. Every week, tape a new friendly note on the inside of your rear window, something like, "Wanda, Great meeting you! I really love your helmet!!! Let's do donuts soon." A bad girl knows that a meter maid is a real person with real feelings who just wants love, respect, and a few dumb jokes like everyone else who works for the city. If you show your meter maid some casual love, she'll show you some leniency.

Ways to Keep the Casual Love Alive

Use Terms of Endearment

Always give your Meter Maid or Meter Man a sweet pet name. Say it loud and proud every chance you get.

Meter Diva	Scooter Pie	Meter Daddy
Meter Dude	Parking Power	Meter Madonna
Meter Dudette	Princess	
M 'n' M	Meter Mama	

end a relationship when you find him in bed with another woman and you wish you

Bring Gifts

* On a hot day, bring your meter man a tall, cold lemonade. (Spike it with a splash of vodka to really get on his bad side!)
* On a cold day, bring your meter mama a steaming mug of hot cocoa. (Spike it with a splash of Kahlúa or Bailey's to warm her up fast!)
* Don't forget birthdays and holidays! Fuzzy dice are always nice. A mini-wreath makes a sweet grille ornament!

Play Friendly Practical Jokes

* Attach tin cans with string to the rear bumper of the scooter and write "Just Kidding" in shaving cream on the back window.
* Slap an "I've Got Butt Pride" or "My Other Car Is a Broom" sticker on the scooter's bumper. (If your meter maid doesn't drive a scooter, just slap a Butt Pride sticker right on her butt! She'll think you're a hoot.)
* Run ahead of her and plug all expired meters with quarters. (Be sure to wink and hold your belly in an exaggerated laugh. Bad girl friends can be such a tease!)
* Secretly swipe her pen and replace it with a disappearing ink pen!

were in bed with her. You know it's time to start a relationship when all of your

Getting Personal with Your Mechanic

Think back to high school . . . Remember how all the brainy babes and the popular girls shunned the auto-shop guys? Guess what? Those guys are now charging you by the hour! Don't panic. Here's your chance to prove that paybacks don't have to be hell. With a little spritz of baddy sauce, you can make paybacks heavenly. All your mechanic really wants is a little respect, a little personal attention, and a lot of food!

Three Gotta Do's

1. Learn your mechanic's first name and use it whenever you stop by or call to make an appointment.
2. Cover a large tin of brownies or cinnamon rolls with foil, place it on your manifold, and drive for 20 to 30 minutes at 45 miles per hour to warm. (Leave it there as an unexpected treat.)
3. Always look and act your baddest. (Dress and act like a single girl on the go.)

Before the Tune-up . . .

* Tie an old bra to your antenna to show your bad girl colors. (Pink, red, or black get the baddest results!)
* Write "Bad Girl" on a pantyliner and slap it on your bumper.
* Leave a few sexy, sassy snapshots of you and your girlfriends tucked in the visor. (No boyfriend photos!)

Things Not to Say to Your Mechanic

* Will you jump me, please?
* In high school, I was super popular.
* Can I watch you jack it up?

* I just won the lottery!
* It kind of smells like a burning rubber.
* That Chicken McNugget in my muffler is supposed to be there.
* Do you really think I need a lube job? I just got some last night.
* I'll have to ask my boyfriend.
* Do you get manicures?

Getting Personal with Your Delivery Guy

He (or she) is your connection to the free world—often your only connection. He wears a uniform. He brings you gifts and asks for your autograph. He wears shorts all year-round. He has a bounce in his step and, some days, he even whistles! Your delivery guy deserves your casual love! If you show your appreciation of him, he'll show you his . . . Oh, who cares if he can actually do anything for you? He's hot.

Whenever he visits your home or office . . .

Welcome him with style:
Sing the "Who wears short shorts?" song.
Offer to apply sunscreen to his lean, lovely legs.

Ask him deep questions:
"Who put the special in Special Delivery? You, baby."
"Wanna go as my date to my father's third wedding?"

Communicate clearly:
Even when you don't need him, you still want him. Put a sign in the window of your home or office that reads "UPS—No. BAD—Yes!"

can't go out with friends without getting guilt-tripped later. You know it's time to

Use Subliminal Badvertising:

When you mean to say "Priority overnight delivery," accidentally say "Priority overnight guest."

When you mean to say "FedEx pickup," accidentally say "SexEd pick-me-up."

Note to Self: Must send yourself more packages!

Getting Personal with Your Bartender

He (or she) is your connection to the free drink world—often your only connection. Learn his first name and always use it. Talk to him like a real friend before you have anything to drink. (Drunken bartender buddies are a dime a dozen.) Tip generously, especially when he buys you a drink. Don't just tell him your sad stories, tell him your bad stories! When you bring him into your bad girl swirl, he'll give you and your personal posse the V.I.P. treatment.

Welcome him with style:

"Hey, handsome! Of all the men I love behind bars, you're my favorite."

Blow him a kiss and whisper, "Give me the unusual, please."

Ask him deep questions:

Smile and wink, "Are your nuts fresh tonight?"

"How much for an unwell drink?"

Communicate clearly:

Always say, "Please, put it on my tab."

Use Subliminal Badvertising:

When you mean to say "Straight up with a twist," accidentally say "Hard up with a twist."

start a relationship when you stop dating yourself and start stalking yourself.

When you mean to say "Hey bartender, make me a bad girl!," accidentally say "Hey bartender, make me your bad girl!"

Getting Personal with Your Dry Cleaner

Sadly, most people overlook the opportunity for a deep and lasting relationship with their dry cleaner. They're in a rush and don't make the time to connect. Think about it. Embarrassing stains and pocket trash, slashed designer labels from sample sales, busted zippers from . . . oh, never mind. Your dry cleaner knows more about you and your lifestyle than your mother! You need your dry cleaner to love you and feel all warm and fuzzy when you walk in the door. If you give her a little casual love rush, she'll squeeze in all your rush jobs.

Welcome her with style:

Along with your bundle, always arrive with a big smile and a small gift (great gift idea—sculpture from metal hangers).

Tell her you love the way her chemicals smell and you'd like to borrow some for perfume.

Ask her deep questions:

"Does the huge electric closet rack have a beginning and an end?"

"Do you use an ultraviolet light to identify bodily fluid stains?"

Communicate clearly:

With each delivery, leave a sweet little note confessing your dry cleaner love in a pocket. (It's a sweet unexpected treat!)

Always attach a note to any stain with your best guess of what it is. Write "mayonnaise stain" in your best handwriting and decorate with a drawing or a smiley face.

Use subliminal badvertising:

When you mean to say, "Dog hair. So much!," accidentally say, "I care. So much!"

When you mean to say, "Will it be ready for me Friday?," accidentally say, "Will you be ready for me Friday?"

How to Say No without Saying "No"

Good girls are raised to do whatever they are asked to do, especially by their family. Poor suckers. Fortunately, a bad girl knows when and how to say "no" evasively with grace and style.

* "I would love to come to dinner with you and the Hendersons! I can't wait to show off my new Mohawk and nose ring."

* "Sure I can loan you $1,000. But I'll have to pay you in quarters. After my audit, this IRS agent is watching my bank account like a sniper."

* "You bet I'll baby-sit again on Saturday night! Perfect timing. My new boyfriend gets out of prison on Friday and he just loves children."

* "Of course I'll help you move! You have disability insurance, don't you? I've been having a little disk problem lately. But hey, no worries. I'll be there!"

* "Yeah, I'll turn down the music, but you'll have to listen to us having sex!"

You know it's time to start a relationship when you can see your kids in his eyes.

Instant Intimate Alias Finder

Can't get past your intimacy issues when trying to get personal? All you need is a good bad girl alias!

	First Name	Last Name	Examples
Your Sex Kitten Name	favorite animal to pet	the last place you did it	Chinchilla Divan Bunny Hot Tub Pussy Dunes
Your Foreign Affair Name	a foreign city where you kissed a stranger	last airline you flew	Paris Virgin Alberta Al Italia Florence Lufthansa
Your Romantic Comedy Name	favorite cartoon character	award you're most likely to win	Annie Emmy Lucy Oscar Veronica Grammy
Your Under-the-Covers Name	how you like your martinis	a hot way to communicate	Dirty Touch Shaken Kiss Twist Whisper

Things to Do with . . . Your Bra

* Hang in kitchen to hold ripening fruit

* Tie to lumber sticking out of the trunk when returning from Home Depot

* Hogtie an unruly guest

* Tie to a cute guy's belt loop at parties to stake your claim

* Write your name and number and discreetly distribute as a personal calling card

* Whip off and tie to a collar for an instant dog leash. Grrr!

* Decorate, shellac until hard, then hang as wall art

* Tie around the old oak tree when waiting for a loved one to return

* Tie to your car antenna and show your Bad Girl colors when on the road

* Tie the trunk shut

* Stuff a black one with cotton and tie around hair like a headband for instant kitten ears. Meow!

* Hang from your window to announce that the Bad Girl is back

* Twin hamster hammock

* Fill bra cups with pudding cups, hang from your front door, and use as welcoming door knocker

You know it's time to end a relationship when he takes the time to cut you out of

Getting Personal with Your Pet

One of the deepest and most rewarding relationships a girl can have is with her dog—or cat or bird or fish. There's no fear of intimacy, no worries about excessive body hair, and no messy sex. No matter what kind of furry, feathery friend you have at home, your pet always wants more quality time, more love, and more heavy petting from you! But that's not all he/she wants. Your pet wants real romance!

Rituals and routines are very important to most pets. They signal that it's time to enter the love zone. To set the mood for romance, follow these five steps, then go where the mood takes you.

1. Pop in a romantic CD.
2. Turn the lights down low.
3. Light a candle or two.
4. Snuggle together on floor pillows, the sofa, or your bed.
5. Make eye contact, tenderly caress his or her face, then playfully feed your pet a few special treats.

(If the moment feels right, a little kiss now can be quite special.)

Fun Things to Do with Your Pet

* Play dress-up. (Your old diaphragm makes a feisty cat cap! A silk scarf makes a fabulous cat cape!)
* Hold him/her in your arms and sing sweet love songs.
* Make matching tiaras with pipe cleaners, cotton balls, and glitter.

all photos. You know it's time to start a relationship when Friday nights are just

* Talk dirty with your parrot.
* Play practical jokes. Write "I'm a bad girl" on a panty-liner and slap it on your dog's back before going out on a walk.
* Remember: Never tease your pooch! If you hint at a juicy French kiss, you must follow through or else your pet will lose trust and confidence. Don't be shy. Your dog's mouth is cleaner than yours!
* Transform your cat into a cat toy. With a little Scotch tape and a few feet of curling ribbon, your cat will be chasing his tail for days!
* Pillow talk. Whisper savory, tender treats to your pet, such as:
  "I think it's so sexy when you sniff butts."
  "Your pink, wet nose drives me wild."
  "When I look into your eyes, I can see myself."

Heavy Petting
Here are some beautiful ways to bond with your pet:
* Dance cheek to cheek or cheek to beak.
* Take a romantic bubble bath with your dog.

the same as any other night, or at least that's what your sock puppet tells you. You

* Swap jewelry. Let your doggy or kitty wear your chic choker while you wear his collar and dog tag. (A great way to feel close when you're off at work!)
* Air-kiss your fish with a soft, open mouth.
* Spoon together on the sofa and watch a DVD.
* Laminate a photo of you and glue it to the bottom of her dog bowl.

Write Pet Poetry

Haiku (5-7-5 syllables) is the perfect way to honor your pet and commemorate a beautiful moment in your relationship. It's short, sweet, easy, and fun! For example:

kissing the new guy
sweet reminder of who's boss
your fur in his mouth

gleeful crotch sniffings
I giggle and stop to think
do I need a bath?

roommate's Zen garden
calming rake repetition
around poop pebbles

know it's time to end a relationship when you realize he's never available on a

Accessorize Your Pet!

* Bandanas are a stylish place to start. But don't stop there! Your precious pooch will feel oh-so-chic at the dog park wearing a little feather boa and tiara.
* Paint your dog's nails a dazzling color that matches yours.

Perfect Pet Gifts

Your Perfect Pet	The Perfect Gift
hamster	an electric treadmill
ferret	a Coach suede handbag (for lunches out together)
snake	sombrero and a bottle of Patrón
dog	a hat, a scarf, and a convertible
cat	a box of tampons (the über-cool feminist cat toy)
rabbit	Kate Spade tote bag (for brunches out together)
bird	a subscription to the *New York Times*
iguana	yoga mat (for sun salutations)

Note to Self: Avoid the relationship path of leash resistance.

Saturday night. You know it's time to start a relationship when you think "old

Boundaries for Brains

Everyone knows that healthy relationships require healthy boundaries. If only all your relationships were healthy! A brainy bad girl knows that even real casual relationships require real creative boundaries.

Invisible Electric Fence: The instant they say a predetermined word, do a predetermined thing, or cross a predetermined line, you electrify them with a shocking jolt of expletives.

Emotional Hula Hoop: With a little practice and a lot of hip action, you can pull them in and push them away all at the same time!

Verbal Towel Snap: Aim for a sensitive soft spot, then fire off a real zinger that smarts!

Barbed Tongue Coral: It's the perfect way to keep all those free-range loonies, horny studs, and mad cows at a safe distance! Don't let them play in your field unless you open the gate.

Mind Condom: Now you can protect your brain as well as your body from any STD (Socially Toxic Diseased) person. Whenever you get physically or emotionally naked, relax! You've got protection.

Plastic Bubble: "Please look but don't touch. I can see you but I can't hear you!" Now every mean thing they say bounces right off and never hurts you! Just be careful not to isolate yourself to death.

maid" sounds kind of hip and street. You know it's time to end a relationship when

Setting Your Relationship Priorities

Getting your relationship house in order calls for setting priorities. Most girls waste time doing things that are not important or urgent, but bad girls know what truly matters now and later.

URGENT AXIS

Urgent but not important:
Finding a date for your
  cousin's wedding
Chocolate
Car sex
Finding a cigarette after
  midnight at a party

Important and urgent:
Finding a condom now!
Feeling self-lust
Shopping
Coming to a bad girl's
  rescue
Booty-call waiting
A smart, sassy comeback

**Not urgent and not
important:**
Finding that boring guy's
  number
Washing the curtains
Filling in your little peri-
  odic chart
Returning that boring
  guy's call

Important but not urgent:
Finding true love
Self-knowledge
Developing a healthy
  lifestyle
Inner peace
A 401K
Drinking 8 glasses of
  water a day

IMPORTANT AXIS

he tells you how great it is that he can treat you "like one of the guys." You know

Choosing Your Battles

When one of your relationships is threatened, it can be hard to know when to let it go and when to let it blow. As a service to bad girls everywhere, the Pink House has issued a new Color-Coded Terrible Behavior System that monitors bad-girl world conditions, denoting a color code for each level of conflict with suggested procedures on how to handle the threat to your personal power safely.

The Situation: Your stay-at-home mother-in-law insults your cooking abilities in front of your husband.

The Alert: Code Eggplant

The Counter Attack: Smile and say, "It really is a shame that my incredibly successful career has hindered my cooking. Good thing I make a LOT of money and can pay someone to cook for me. More mediocre lasagna?"

The Situation: Your bad girl friend is 40 minutes late for lunch. Again.

The Alert: Code Tangerine

The Counter Attack: Order the most expensive dish on the menu and enjoy it. When she arrives carrying shopping bags, tell her she should definitely get the same, then excuse yourself for a moment. On your way out the door, tell the waitress that your friend will take the check and be on your merry, well-fed way. (Payback's a bitch!)

The Situation: Your so-called bad girl friend walks into a bar with your so-called boyfriend on her arm.

The Alert: Code Pink

The Counter Attack: Slowly rise from your bar stool with

it's time to start a relationship when you refer to being single as your "condition."

CODE ALERT!!!

Alert Color	Threat Condition	Counter Attack Strategy
CODE PINK	Severe	No matter where you are or what the situation, dramatically throw a drink in the enemy's face.
CODE FUCHSIA	Critical	Calls for flashy, eye-catching bad girl action that stands out in a crowded room.
CODE TANGERINE	Serious	Calls for a juicy bad girl intervention with sticky-sweet revenge.
CODE EGGPLANT	Guarded	Unsavory behavior that doesn't hurt that much but leaves a nasty purple shiner. An icy comeback will decrease your swelling anger.
CODE BEET	Normal	Unpleasant situation that makes you turn beet red. You're strongly advised to ignore it, rise above the bad behavior, and find a savvy way to get revenge.

You know it's time to end a relationship when you're staying together just because

your drink in one hand and your neighbor's drink in the other. Approach the enemies calmly and say, "Would you like a drink?" When they say yes, say, "It's on me." Then throw a drink in each of their faces and follow up with, "Oh wait, I guess it's on you!"

The Situation: Your boss takes credit for your brilliant idea in a staff meeting.
The Alert: Code Beet
The Counter Attack: Think about all of the wicked things you'd like to say to her and then don't. Next time she asks to pick your brain, enthusiastically give her your lamest ideas, then send out a group memo highlighting your best ideas with your name attached.

The Situation: Your neighbor continues to let her doggie doo on your front walk and doesn't pick it up. On your way to work, you step in it, ruining your new pumps.
The Alert: Code Fuchsia
The Counter Attack: Scoop it up with her *New York Times,* wrap the whole package in a brown paper bag with a fuchsia bow, and leave it outside her apartment door with a note that says, "Thought you might enjoy a doggie bag."

The Situation: Your boss laughingly insults you in a staff meeting . . . again!
The Alert: Code Pink
The Counter Attack: Stand up, calmly grab your cup of tepid coffee, and dump it in her lap. Enough is enough. Proudly leave the room with a big smile on your face and immediately empty out your desk.

rents are so expensive. You know it's time to start a relationship when you've gone

How to Be a Badder Neighbor

* Pick up the Sunday paper in your sexiest lingerie or nothing at all.

* Set up a lemonade-and-vodka stand in front of your house every evening at cocktail hour.

* Invite your neighbors to all your parties—and invite yourself to all of theirs!

* Leave the shades up when you get undressed.

* Bowl with frozen Cornish game hens in the hallway late at night.

* On recycling day, build pyramids with your neighbors' bottles and cans. (Be sure to give an award to the biggest drinkers!)

* Start racy rumors about yourself by talking into the bathroom vent.

* Give a cute neighbor fresh-cut flowers cut from another neighbor's garden.

* Leave your favorite cute neighbor a set of keys to your place (just in case you get locked out, of course!).

an entire month without even thinking about your ex. You know it's time to end a

Life is short—love hard!

Congratulations, you're a super bad girl. Now give your-self a big wet kiss, a full-body hug, and a loving smack on the ass. You deserve it! You've got the hip action to turn heads and the lip action to speak your mind and change the world.

Pssst. Remember—you've got to give personal to get personal. So don't be stingy with the You Goo.

Now get out there and strut your bad-girl stuff, spread some love, and make the world a badder place. Be sure to stay strong, safe, fearless, funny—and take very detailed notes for your memoirs.

Note to self: When closing a book, always open a bottle of champagne.

relationship when he becomes best buddies with your previously hated ex.

About the Author

Cameron Tuttle is the original bad girl and the author of the best-selling *The Bad Girl's Guide to the Open Road, The Bad Girl's Guide to Getting What You Want,* and *The Bad Girl's Guide to the Party Life,* as well as *The Paranoid's Pocket Guide,* all from Chronicle Books. She lives, loves, and works badly in San Francisco.

About the Illustrator

Susannah Bettag is a very bad girl. Her bad illustrations have appeared in all the *Bad Girl's Guides* as well as in many magazines. She lives but rarely sleeps in San Francisco.

Go to **badgirlswirl.com** to reach the author and illustrator and to mix it up with other bad girls.

Other bad girl products:

The Bad Girl's Guide to the Open Road
The Bad Girl's Guide to Getting What You Want
The Bad Girl's Guide to the Party Life

The Bad Girl's Little Pink Book
The Bad Girl's Engagement Calendar
The Bad Girl's Rage-a-Day Calendar
The Bad Girl's Power Planner
The Bad Girl's Scrappy Book
Me and My Bad Girls Photo Album
Be a Bad Girl: A Journal
Greetings From a Bad Girl: 30 Assorted Postcards
The Bad Girl's Valentines
The Bad Girl's Sticky Notes
The Bad Girl's Brag Book
The Bad Girl's Social Whirl Door Sign
The Bad Girl's Calling Cards
The Bad Girl's Rate-Your-Date Journal